Active Learning

Active Learning

101 Strategies to Teach Any Subject

MEL SILBERMAN

Temple University

Allyn and Bacon
Boston   London   Toronto   Sydney   Tokyo   Singapore

Copyright © 1996 by Allyn & Bacon
A Simon & Schuster Company
Needham Heights, Massachusetts 02194

Library of Congress Cataloging-in-Publication Data

Silberman, Melvin L.
    Active Learning : 101 strategies to teach any subject / by Mel
Silberman.
        p.   cm.
    Includes bibliographical references.
    ISBN 0-205-17866-9
    1. Active learning.   2. Activity programs in education.   3. Team
learning approach in education.   4. Learning, Psychology of.
I. Title.
LB1027.23.S556   1996
370.15´23—dc20   95-44838
                                                                          CIP

Printed in the United States of America
10 9 8 7   00 99 98

Contents

Preface   ix

About the Author   xv

Acknowledgments   xvii

1 Introducing Active Learning   1

How the Brain Works   2
Learning Styles   4
The Social Side of Learning   5
Concerns about Active Learning   6
The Nuts and Bolts of Active Learning   9

2 How to Get Students Active from the Start   32

Team-Building Strategies   34
1. Trading Places   35
2. Who's in the Class?   36
3. Group Résumé   38
4. Predictions   40
5. TV Commercial   41
6. The Company You Keep   42
7. Really Getting Acquainted   44
8. Team Getaway   45
9. Reconnecting   46
10. The Great Wind Blows   47
11. Setting Class Ground Rules   48

On-the-Spot Assessment Strategies   50
12. Assessment Search   51
13. Questions Students Have   52
14. Instant Assessment   53
15. A Representative Sample   54
16. Class Concerns   55

Immediate Learning Involvement Strategies   56
17. Active Knowledge Sharing   57
18. Rotating Trio Exchange   59
19. Go to Your Post   61
20. Lightening the Learning Climate   62
21. Exchanging Viewpoints   63

95812

22. True or False?   64

23. Buying into the Course   65

3   How to Help Students Acquire Knowledge, Skills, and Attitudes . . . Actively   67

Full-Class Learning   **70**

24. Inquiring Minds Want to Know   71

25. Listening Teams   72

26. Guided Note-Taking   73

27. Lecture Bingo   75

28. Synergetic Teaching   76

29. Guided Teaching   77

30. Meet the Guests   78

31. Acting Out   79

32. What's My Line?   80

33. Video Critic   82

Stimulating Class Discussion   **83**

34. Active Debate   84

35. Town Meeting   86

36. Three-Stage Fishbowl Discussion   87

37. Expanding Panel   89

38. Point–Counterpoint   90

39. Reading Aloud   91

40. Trial by Jury   92

Prompting Questions   **93**

41. Learning Starts with a Question   94

42. Planted Questions   96

43. Role Reversal Questions   98

Collaborative Learning   **99**

44. Information Search   100

45. The Study Group   101

46. Card Sort   103

47. Learning Tournament   104

48. The Power of Two   106

49. Team Quiz   107

Peer Teaching   **108**

50. Group-to-Group Exchange   109

51. Jigsaw Learning   111

52. Everyone Is a Teacher Here   113

53. Peer Lessons   114

54. Student-Created Case Studies   116

55. In the News   118

56. Poster Session   119

Independent Learning **121**
  57. Imagine   122
  58. Writing in the Here and Now   124
  59. Mind Maps   126
  60. Action Learning   127
  61. Learning Journals   129
  62. Learning Contracts   130

Affective Learning **132**
  63. Seeing How It Is   133
  64. Billboard Ranking   135
  65. What? So What? Now What?   136
  66. Active Self-Assessment   138
  67. Role Models   140

Skill Development **141**
  68. The Firing Line   142
  69. Active Observation and Feedback   144
  70. Nonthreatening Role Playing   146
  71. Triple Role Playing   147
  72. Rotating Roles   148
  73. Modeling the Way   149
  74. Silent Demonstration   150
  75. Practice-Rehearsal Pairs   152
  76. I Am the _____   153
  77. Curveballs   154
  78. Advisory Group   155

4 How to Make Learning Unforgettable   156

Reviewing Strategies **158**
  79. Index Card Match   159
  80. Topical Review   160
  81. Giving Questions and Getting Answers   161
  82. Crossword Puzzle   162
  83. Jeopardy Review   163
  84. College Bowl   165
  85. Student Recap   166
  86. Bingo Review   167
  87. Hollywood Squares   169

Self-Assessment **170**
  88. Reconsidering   171
  89. Return on Your Investment   172
  90. Gallery of Learning   173
  91. Physical Self-Assessment   174
  92. Assessment Collage   176

Future Planning   **177**

93. Keep On Learning   178
94. Bumper Stickers   179
95. I Hereby Resolve   180
96. Follow-Up Questionnaire   181
97. Sticking to It   183

Final Sentiments   **185**

98. Goodbye Scrabble   186
99. Connections   187
100. Class Photo   188
101. The Final Exam   189

Preface

*You can tell students what they need to know very fast.
But they will forget what you tell them even faster.*

Yes, there is a whole lot more to teaching than telling! Learning is not an automatic consequence of pouring information into a student's head. It requires the learner's own mental involvement and doing. Explanation and demonstration, by themselves, will never lead to real, lasting learning. Only learning that is *active* will do this.

What makes learning "active"? When learning is active, students do most of the work. They use their brains . . . studying ideas, solving problems, and applying what they learn. Active learning is fast-paced, fun, supportive, and personally engaging. Often, students are out of their seats, moving about and thinking aloud.

Why is it necessary to make learning active? To learn something well, it helps to hear it, see it, ask questions about it, and discuss it with others. Above all, students need to "do it"—figure things out by themselves, come up with examples, try out skills, and do assignments that depend on the knowledge they already have or must acquire.

We know that students learn best by doing. But how do we promote active learning? **This book contains specific, practical strategies that can be used for almost any subject matter.** They are designed to enliven your classroom. Some are a lot of fun and some are downright serious, but they all are intended to deepen learning and retention.

Active Learning brings together in one source a comprehensive collection of instructional strategies. It includes ways to get students active from the start through activities that build teamwork and immediately get them thinking about the subject matter. There are also techniques for conducting full-class learning and small-group learning, stimulating discussion and debate, practicing skills, prompting questions, and even getting the students to teach each other. Finally, there are methods for reviewing what's been learned, assessing how one has changed, and considering the next steps to take so that the learning sticks.

Active Learning is for anyone, experienced or novice, who teaches technical or nontechnical information, concepts, and skills. Although many of the strategies and tips apply to teachers at any level, the book is directed to those who teach older children and adults. Teachers in middle schools, high schools, colleges, and centers for adult education will find this collection especially useful.

Thanks to the influence of Piaget, Montessori, and others, teachers of early childhood and elementary education have long practiced active learning. They know that young children learn best from concrete, activity-based experiences. Even those teachers who are not mindful of the facts of child development make learning an active affair. They have learned that children's attention span is short and their ability to sit still is limited. To compensate, they keep children active and moving about.

Yet, with older students, there is a tendency to suspend high levels of active learning. Almost all teachers, from middle school on up to higher education, pepper their classrooms with occasional discussion and question-and-answer sessions. Some include games, role playing, and even small-group learning activities from time to time. But the commitment to active, lively learning is short-lived. Why?

You can probably think of many reasons. For example, teachers tend to teach the way they have been taught, and the chalk talk model is what we all grew up on. Beyond that, there is a default assumption that mature learners don't require heightened activity and a fast pace to learn effectively. Because the developed mind is capable of reflection, perspective taking, and abstract thought, some teachers assume that older students are really learning as they sit listening to the lesson. This belief is usually strong enough to last even when teachers are disappointed with how much is retained and how little is applied. Maybe things were better in the past, but today's students are products of an MTV world of sights as well as sounds, movement as well as meditation. Moreover, there is a far greater diversity of students these days—diverse not only in gender, race, and ethnicity, but also in their styles of learning. Active learning is needed not only to add excitement but also to show respect for individual differences and multiple intelligences.

Another reason that learning is not active enough when students are older is that teachers feel bound by their subject matter and pressured by the limited time they have to teach it. The idea that learning is separated into distinct subject areas has persisted for centuries and is not likely to go away easily. Although the conditions of the postmodern world are calling into question traditional forms of schooling and curricular design, it is still difficult to convince most administrators and parents that "covering" the subject matter has limited value. Furthermore, the belief persists that active learning takes too much time—it may be nice in theory but unrealistic in practice.

Perhaps the biggest reason why active learning is not the hallmark of schools for older children and adults is that there has not been enough **concrete advice** about how to install it in any classroom. A few excellent books that have been published recently suggest, in general terms, how to incorporate case studies, simulations, group learning, projects, and other participatory methods into high schools and colleges. When I have shown these books to interested teachers, many have asked me to spell out specific strategies that could apply to their subject matter. That is why I have compiled *Active Learning.* It is filled with practical methods, with step-by-step instructions.

Active Learning begins with a chapter on "Introducing Active Learning." I will not only discuss the dismal track record of passive forms of teaching but also explain how our understanding of how the mind works when learning demands an active approach to classroom instruction. The chapter continues with a discussion of student learning styles, the social side of learning, and the common concerns teachers have about introducing active learning into their classrooms. The chapter concludes with over 100 tips to start you off on organizing and facilitating active learning. Included are ways to form groups, obtain participation, create classroom layouts, facilitate discussion, and more!

The 101 techniques described throughout the remainder of *Active Learning* are concrete strategies that enable you to apply active learning to your subject matter. These techniques are divided into three sections, as follows.

How to Get Students Active from the Start

This section contains icebreakers and other opening activities for any kind of class. The techniques are designed to do one or more of the following:

- *Team building:* Helping students to become acquainted with each other or creating a spirit of cooperation and interdependence
- *On-the-spot assessment:* Learning about students' attitudes, knowledge, and experience of students
- *Immediate learning involvement:* Creating initial interest in the subject matter

In addition, these techniques encourage students to take an active role right from the beginning.

How to Help Students Acquire Knowledge, Skills, and Attitudes ... Actively

This section contains instructional techniques that can be used when you are at the heart of your lesson. The techniques are designed to avoid or reinforce teacher-led instruction. A wide range of alternatives are provided, all of which gently push students to think, feel, and apply. They include:

- *Full-class learning:* Teacher-led instruction that stimulates the entire class
- *Class discussion:* Dialogue and debate of key issues
- *Question prompting:* Student requests for clarification
- *Collaborative learning:* Assignments done cooperatively in small groups of students
- *Peer teaching:* Instruction led by students
- *Independent learning:* Learning activities performed individually
- *Affective learning:* Activities that help students to examine their feelings, values, and attitudes
- *Skill development:* Learning and practicing skills, both technical and nontechnical

How to Make Learning Unforgettable

This section contains ways to conclude a class so that the student reflects on what he or she has learned and considers how to apply it in the future. The focus is not on what you have told them, but what they take away. The techniques are designed to do one or more of the following:

- *Review:* Recalling and summarizing what has been learned
- *Self-assessment:* Evaluating changes in knowledge, skills, or attitudes
- *Future planning:* Determining how the student will continue the learning after the class is over
- *Expression of final sentiments:* Communicating the thoughts, feelings, and concerns students have at the end

Each of the 101 techniques you are about to read is described and illustrated in the following ways:

- *Overview:* A statement about the purpose of the technique and the setting in which it is appropriate
- *Procedure:* Step-by-step instructions and illustrations to show you how to use the technique and apply it to your subject matter
- *Variations:* Suggestions for alternative ways to use the technique

One Final Word

Use these techniques as is or adapt them to fit your needs. Add your own creativity! As you do, bear in mind these suggestions:

- Don't experiment wildly. Try out a new method no more than once a week.
- When you introduce a method to students, sell it as an alternative to the usual way of doing things that you think might be worth a try. Obtain their feedback.
- Don't overload students with too many activities. *Less is often more.* Use just a few to enliven your class.
- Make your instructions crystal clear. Demonstrate or illustrate what students are expected to do so that there is no confusion that might distract them from getting the most out of the technique.

Good luck!

About the Author

Dr. Mel Silberman is Professor of Psychological Studies in Education at Temple University, where he specializes in instructional psychology. He has an international reputation in the field of active learning.

He is the author of the following books:

The Experience of Schooling (Holt, Rinehart and Winston, 1969)
The Psychology of Open Teaching and Learning (Little, Brown, 1972)
Real Learning (Little, Brown, 1976)
How to Discipline without Feeling Guilty (Dutton, 1980; Research Press, 1981)
Confident Parenting (Warner, 1988)
Active Training (Lexington, 1990)
20 Active Training Programs, Vol. I (Pfeiffer, 1992)
20 Active Training Programs, Vol II (Pfeiffer, 1994)
101 Ways to Make Training Active (Pfeiffer, 1995)
When Your Child is Difficult (Research Press, 1995)

Under the auspices of Active Training in Princeton, New Jersey (609-924-8157), Dr. Silberman has conducted active learning seminars for preservice and inservice teachers, adult educators, college instructors, and workplace trainers in hundreds of educational, governmental, human service, and business organizations.

Dr. Silberman is a graduate of Brandeis University and holds an A.M. and a Ph.D. in educational psychology from The University of Chicago.

Acknowledgments

Over the past twenty-five years, I have had the exhilarating experience of working with preservice and inservice teachers at all levels of education. Thousands of you have tried out active learning techniques and have given me a vote of confidence to keep on developing more. I appreciate the many educators who have engaged in this experimentation and have given me the gift of your encouragement and constructive feedback.

I also am grateful for the contributions of Rebecca Birch, Cynthia Denton-Ade, and Sivasailam Thiagarajan. They willingly shared with me their active learning ideas in recent years and graciously agreed to let me include several of them in this collection.

I wish to acknowledge several of my graduate students at Temple University who have assisted me in compiling *Active Learning*. Craig Loundas was particularly helpful in the development of this book. Also, this book would not have been possible without the assistance of Karen Lawson. Thank you.

Finally, I want to thank Richard Maurer of the Tuckahoe Public Schools, Eastchester, New York; Paul H. Westmeyer of the University of Texas, San Antonio; and Frank Taylor of Pollard Middle School in Needham, Massachusetts, for reviewing the manuscript.

Throughout my professional life, my wife, Shoshana, has been a constant source of creative ideas, inspiration, and love. A superb educator in her own right, she is an invaluable sounding board, with an uncanny knack of sensing when I'm on the mark and when I am off. One could not have a more "active" partner.

1

Introducing Active Learning

Over 2400 years ago, Confucius declared:

What I **hear,** I forget.

What I **see,** I remember.

What I **do,** I understand.

These three simple statements speak volumes about the need for active learning.

I have modified and expanded the wisdom of Confucius into what I call the Active Learning Credo.

What I **hear,** I forget.

What I hear and **see,** I remember a little.

What I hear, see, and **ask questions about** or **discuss** with someone else, I begin to understand.

What I hear, see, discuss, and **do,** I acquire knowledge and skill.

What I **teach** to another, I master.

Why do I make these statements?

There are several reasons that most people tend to forget what they hear. One of the most interesting reasons has to do with the rate at which a teacher speaks and the rate at which students listen.

Most teachers speak about 100 to 200 words per minute. But how many of those words do students hear? Well, it depends on how they are listening. If the students are really concentrating, they might be able to listen attentively to about 50 or 100 words per minute, or half of what a teacher is saying. That's because students are thinking a lot while they are listening. It's hard to keep up with a talkative teacher. More likely, the students are not concentrating because, even if the material is interesting, it is hard to concentrate for a sustained period of time. Studies show that students hear (without thinking) at the rate of 400 to 500 words per minute. When listening for a sustained period of time to a teacher who is talking up to four times more slowly, students are likely to get bored, and their minds will wander.

1

In fact, one study demonstrates that students in lecture-based college classrooms are not attentive about 40 percent of the time (Pollio, 1984). Moreover, while students retain 70 percent in the first ten minutes of a lecture, they retain only 20 percent of the last ten minutes (McKeachie, 1986). No wonder students in a lecture-based introductory psychology course knew only 8 percent more than a control group who had never taken the course at all (Rickard et al., 1988). Imagine what the results would be in a high school or middle school class!

Two well-known figures in the cooperative education movement, David and Roger Johnson, along with Karl Smith, point out several problems with sustained lecturing (Johnson, Johnson, & Smith, 1991):

- Student attention decreases with each passing minute.

- It appeals only to auditory learners.

- It tends to promote lower level learning of factual information.

- It assumes that all students need the same information and at the same pace.

- Students tend not to like it.

Adding visuals to a lesson increases retention from 14 to 38 percent (Pike, 1989). Studies have also shown an improvement of up to 200 percent when vocabulary is taught using visual aids! Moreover, the time required to present a concept is reduced up to 40 percent when visuals are used to augment a verbal presentation. A picture may not be worth a thousand words, but it is three times more effective than words alone.

When teaching has both an auditory and a visual dimension, the message is reinforced by two systems of delivery. Also, some students, as we will discuss later, prefer one mode of delivery over the other. By using both, you have a greater chance of meeting the needs of several types of students. But, **merely hearing something and seeing it is not enough to learn it.**

How the Brain Works

Our brain does not function the way an audio- or videotape recorder does. Incoming information is continually being questioned. Our brain asks questions like these:

Have I heard or seen this information before?

Where does this information fit? What can I do with it?

Can I assume that this is the same idea I had yesterday or last month or last year?

The brain doesn't just receive information—it *processes* it.

To process information effectively, it helps to carry out such reflection externally as well as internally. If we discuss information with others and if we are invited to ask questions about it, our brains can do a better job of learning. For example, Ruhl, Hughes, and Schloss (1987) asked students to discuss with a partner what a teacher presented at frequent intervals during the class. Compared to students in a control class for whom there were no pauses for discussion, these students received up to two letter grades higher.

Better yet, if we can *do* something with the information, we can obtain feedback about how well we understand. According to John Holt (1967), learning is enhanced if students are asked to do the following:

1. State the information in their own words.

2. Give examples of it.

3. Recognize it in various guises and circumstances.

4. See connections between it and other facts or ideas.

5. Make use of it in various ways.

6. Foresee some of its consequences.

7. State its opposite or converse.

In many ways, the brain is like a computer, and we are its users. A computer, of course, needs to be "on" in order to work. Our brain needs to be "on" as well. When learning is passive, the brain isn't "on." A computer needs the right software to interpret the data that is input. Our brain needs to link what we are being taught with what we already know and how we think. When learning is passive, the brain doesn't make these links to the software of our minds. Finally, a computer cannot retain information that it has processed without "saving" it. Our brain needs to test the information, recap it, or explain it to someone else in order to store it in its memory banks. When learning is passive, the brain doesn't save what has been presented.

What occurs when teachers flood students with their own thoughts (however insightful and well organized they are) or when they rely too often on "let me show you how" demonstrations and explanations? Pouring facts and concepts into students' heads and masterfully performing skills and procedures actually interferes with learning. The presentation may make an immediate impression on the brain; but, without a photographic memory, students simply cannot retain very much for any period of time.

Of course, real learning is not memorization anyway. Most of what we memorize is lost in hours. Learning can't be swallowed whole. To retain what has been taught, students must chew on it. A teacher cannot do the mental work for students because they must put together what they hear and see into a meaningful whole. Without the opportunity to discuss, ask questions, do, and perhaps even teach someone else, real learning will not occur.

Further, learning is not a one-shot event. Learning comes in waves. It takes several exposures to material to chew on it long enough to understand it. It also takes different kinds of exposures, not just a repetition of input. For example, math can be taught with concrete aids, through workbook exercises, and with daily practical activities. Each way of presenting a concept shapes students' understanding. Even more important is the way in which the exposure happens. If it happens *to* the learner, there will be little mental engagement *by* the learner. When learning is passive, the learner comes to the encounter without curiosity, without questions, and without interest in the outcome (except, perhaps, in the grade he or she will receive.) When learning is active, the learner is *seeking* something. He or she wants an answer to a question, needs information to solve a problem, or is searching for a way to do a job.

Learning Styles

Educators have come to realize that learners come in different styles. Some students learn best by seeing someone else do it. Usually, they like carefully sequenced presentations of information. They prefer to write down what a teacher tells them. During class, they are generally quiet and seldom distracted by noise. These *visual* learners contrast with *auditory* learners, who often do not bother to look at what a teacher does, or to take notes. They rely on their ability to hear and remember. During class, they may be talkative and are easily distracted by noise. *Kinesthetic* learners learn mainly by direct involvement in activity. They tend to be impulsive, with little patience. During class, they may be fidgety unless they can move about and *do*. Their approach to learning can appear haphazard and random.

Of course, few students are exclusively one kind of learner. Grinder (1991) notes that in every group of 30 students, an average of 22 are able to learn effectively as long as a teacher provides a blend of visual, auditory, and kinesthetic activity. The remaining 8 students, however, prefer one of the modalities over the other two so strongly that they struggle to understand the subject matter unless special care is taken to present it in their preferred mode. In order to meet these needs, teaching has to be multisensory and filled with variety.

Educators also have been noticing changes in their students' learning styles. For the past fifteen years, Schroeder and his colleagues (1993) have been giving the Myers-Briggs type Indicator (MBTI) to incoming college students. The MBTI is one of the most widely used instruments in education and business today. It has been especially useful for understanding the role of individual differences in the learning process. Their results indicate that approximately 60 percent of entering students have a *practical* rather than a *theoretical* orientation toward learning, and the percentage grows year by year. Students prefer to be involved with immediate, direct, concrete experiences rather than learning basic concepts first and applying them later on. Other MBTI research, Schroeder points out, shows that high school students prefer learning activity that is *concrete active* to activity that is *abstract reflective* by a ratio of five to one. From all this, he concludes that active modes of teaching and learning create the best match for today's students. To be effective, teachers should use all the following: small-group discussion and projects, in-class presentations and debates, experiential exercises, field experiences, simulations, and case studies. In particular, Schroeder emphasizes, today's students "adapt quite well to group activities and collaborative learning."

These findings come as no surprise if you consider the active pace of modern life. Students today grow up in a world where things happen quickly and where many choices are presented. Sounds come in clever "bites," and colors are vibrant and compelling. Objects, both real and virtual, move quickly. The opportunity to change things from one state to another is everywhere.

The Social Side of Learning

Because today's students face a world of exploding knowledge, rapid change, and uncertainty, they can be anxious and defensive. Abraham Maslow taught us that human beings have within them two sets of forces or needs—one that strives for growth and one that clings to safety. A person who must choose between these two needs will choose safety over growth. The need to feel secure must be met before the need to reach out, take risks, and explore the new can be entertained. Growth forward takes place in little steps, according to Maslow, and "each step forward is made possible by the feeling of being safe, of operating out into the unknown from a safe home port" (Maslow, 1968).

One of the key ways to attain a feeling of safety and security is to be connected to other people and to feel included in a group. This feeling of belonging enables students to face the challenges before them. When they are learning with others rather than alone, they have available the emotional and intellectual support that allows them to go beyond their present level of knowledge and skill.

Jerome Bruner recognizes the social side of learning in his classic book *Toward a Theory of Instruction*. He describes "a deep human need to respond to others and to operate jointly with them toward an objective," which he calls *reciprocity*. Bruner maintains that reciprocity is a source of motivation that any teacher can tap to stimulate learning. He writes: "Where joint action is needed, where reciprocity is required for the group to attain an objective, then there seem to be processes that carry the individual along into learning, sweep him into a competence that is required in the setting of the group" (Bruner, 1966).

These concepts of Maslow and Bruner underlie the development of the collaborative learning methods so popular in educational circles today. Placing students in groups and giving them tasks in which they depend on each other to complete the work is a wonderful way to capitalize on the social needs of students. They tend to become more engaged in learning because they are doing it with their peers. Once involved, they also have a need to talk about what they are experiencing with others, which leads to further connections.

Collaborative learning activities help to drive active learning. Although independent study and full-class instruction also stimulate active learning, the ability to teach through small-group cooperative activities will enable you to promote active learning in a special way. What a student discusses with others and what a student teaches others enable him or her to acquire understanding and master learning. The best collaborative learning methods, such as so-called jigsaw lessons, meet these requirements. Giving different assignments to different students prompts students not only to learn together but also to teach each other.

Concerns about Active Learning

Despite the arguments I have used to support active learning, many teachers are still apprehensive about it. If you share any of their concerns, I hope my responses are helpful.

➡ *Is active learning just a bunch of "fun and games"?*

No, it's not just fun, although learning can be fun and still be worthwhile. Actually, many active learning techniques present students with unusual challenges that require much hard work.

➡ *Does active learning focus so much on activity for its own sake that students don't reflect on what they are learning?*

This is a real concern. Much of the value of active learning comes from thinking about the activities when they are over and discussing their meaning with others. Don't overlook this fact. *Active Learning* includes many suggestions to help students reflect on what they have experienced. It is often valuable to offer a short lesson after an active learning activity to connect what students have experienced to the concepts you want to get across.

➡ *Doesn't active learning require a lot of time? How can you cover course material using active learning methods?*

There is no question that active learning takes more time than straight teaching, but there are many ways to avoid a needless waste of time. Furthermore, even though a lecture can cover considerable ground, one has to question how much students really learn. Lecturers have a tendency to cover the waterfront by throwing in everything possible about a given subject. After all, they reason, you only get one shot at these students, so you'd better make sure to cover it all. Classrooms where learning is active, however, have a lean curriculum and limited goals. The teachers who guide these classrooms understand that students will forget far more than they remember. When the content level is kept moderate, the teacher has time to provide activities that introduce, present, apply, and reflect on what is being learned.

➡ *Can active learning methods spice up dry, uninteresting information?*

Absolutely! Interesting subjects are easy to teach. When a subject is dry, often the mere excitement of active learning methods catches up with students and motivates them to master even boring material.

➡ *When you use groups in active learning, how do you prevent the groups from wasting time and being unproductive?*

Groups can be unproductive when there has been little team building in the beginning of the class and when group work is not carefully structured from the outset. Students become confused about what to do, organize themselves poorly, and get easily off task. Or they may do the work as quickly as possible, skimming the surface rather than digging into the material. There are several ways to teach students how to learn in groups, such as assigning roles to group members, establishing group ground rules, practicing group skills, and so forth. Many tips and techniques in *Active Learning* are geared to this problem.

➡ *Can you "group students to death" using active learning?*

Yes, it can happen. Some teachers overuse groups. They don't give students enough chances to learn things individually, and they don't bring the entire class together enough for teaching and discussion. The key is variety. Variety of learning modalities is the spice of good teaching. Several techniques in *Active Learning* will give you alternatives to small-group learning.

➡ *Is there a danger that students will misinform each other in group-based active learning methods?*

I suppose there is some danger of that, but the advantages of giving learning a social side far outweigh the disadvantages. Anyway, a teacher can always review material with the entire class after student-active attempts to learn it on their own and teach it to each other.

➡ *I'm sold on active learning, but I wonder if my students will be?*

The less accustomed they are to active learning, the more uneasy they will be initially. They may be used to watching the teacher do all the work, sitting back, and believing that they have learned something and will retain it. Some students will complain that active learning is a waste of time. They may prefer well-organized, efficient delivery of information, or they may be anxious about learning by discovery and self-exploration. In the long run, they will benefit from active learning as much as anyone else. In the short run, they will be less anxious if you introduce active learning gradually. Otherwise, you may meet considerable resistance.

➡ *Doesn't it require more preparation and creativity to teach using active learning methods?*

Yes and no. Once you get the hang of it, the extra preparation and creativity will not feel like a burden. You will feel excited about your teaching, and this energy will transfer to your students' learning. Until then, you should find that creating ideas for active learning can be challenging. At first, you will wonder how in the world can you teach certain topics actively! This, of course, is where *Active Learning* comes in. It is intended to ease the transition by providing you with several concrete ways to build activity, variety, and participation into your classroom. As you read each technique, suggestions are given about how to plug in your subject matter. I believe these techniques are useful for virtually any subject matter. As you navigate each technique, however, avoid being a passive reader. Identify a topic you are currently teaching or anticipate teaching in the future, and keep it in mind as you read. By maintaining a problem-solving mind set rather than an information-receiving one, you will be an active reader and on your way to becoming an active teacher.

The Nuts and Bolts of Active Learning

Before reading the 101 active learning strategies described in this book, you may find it useful to consider what I call the nuts and bolts of active learning. I have developed some quick tips for organizing and facilitating active learning to help teachers identify, at a glance, several choices available to them at different points in the course of promoting active learning. Many of these ideas are well known, and you already may be using several of them. But I hope that having an organized list of them will make your job of facilitating active learning easier. Think of these lists as teaching menus from which you can select the option you need at any given moment to make learning active.

Ten Layouts for Setting Up a Classroom

The physical environment in a classroom can make or break active learning. No one setup is ideal, but there are many options to choose from. The "interior decorating" of active learning is fun and chal-

lenging (especially when the furniture is less than ideal). In some cases, furniture can be easily rearranged to create different setups. Even traditional desks can be grouped together to form tables and other arrangements. If you choose to do so, ask students to help move desks, tables, and chairs. That gets them "active," too.

Most of the layouts described here are not meant to be permanent arrangements. If your furniture is movable, it should be possible to use a few of these layouts as you see fit. You will also find suggestions on how to utilize even the most traditional classroom environments for active learning.

1. **U shape:** This is an all-purpose setup. The students have a reading/writing surface, can see you and/or a visual medium easily, and are in face-to-face contact with each other. It's also easy to pair up students, especially when there are two seats per table. The arrangement is ideal for distributing learning handouts quickly to students because you can enter the U and walk to different points with sets of materials.

   You can set up desks, desk chairs, or tables in a squared-off U:

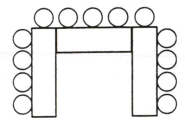

   Be sure there is enough perimeter space in the room so that subgroups of three or more students can pull back from the desks or tables and face each other.

   You can also arrange chairs, desks, or oblong tables in a U that appears more like a semicircle.

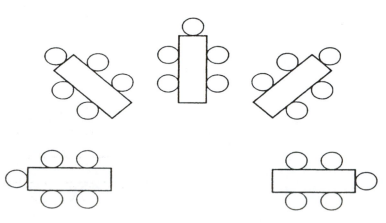

2. **Team-style:** Grouping circular or oblong tables around the class-room enables you to promote team interaction. You can place seats fully around the tables for the most intimate setting. If you do, some students will have to turn their chairs around to face the front of the room to see you, a flipchart/blackboard, or a screen.

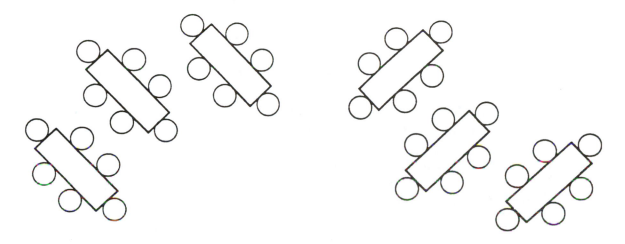

Or you can place seats halfway around so that no student has his or her back to the front of the room.

3. **Conference table:** It's best if the table is relatively circular or square. This arrangement minimizes the importance of the teacher and maximizes the importance of the class. A rectangular table can create a feeling of formality if the teacher is at the head of the table.

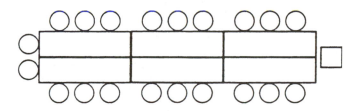

If the teacher sits in the middle of a wider side, the students on the ends will feel left out.

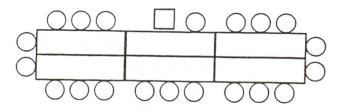

You can form a conference table arrangement by joining together several smaller tables (the center will usually be hollow).

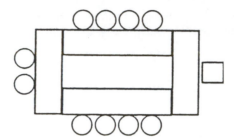

4. **Circle:** Simply seating students in a circle without desks or tables promotes the most direct fact-to-face interaction. A circle is ideal for full-group discussion. Assuming there is enough perimeter space, you can ask students to arrange their chairs quickly into many subgroup arrangements.

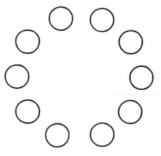

If you want to have a writing surface available for students, use a peripheral arrangement. Have them turn their chairs around when you want group discussion.

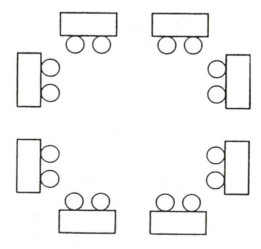

5. **Group on group:** This arrangement allows you to conduct fish-bowl discussions (see page 17) or to set up role-plays, debates, or observations of group activity. The most typical design consists of two concentric circles of chairs. Or you can place a meeting table in the middle, surrounded by an outer ring of chairs.

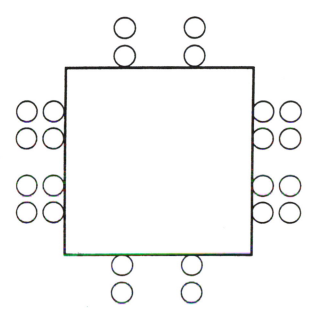

6. **Workstations:** This arrangement is appropriate for an active, labo-ratory-type environment in which each student is seated at a station to perform a procedure or task (e.g., computing, operating a machine, conducting lab work) right after it is demonstrated. A terrific way to encourage learning partnerships (see page 17) is to place two students at the same station.

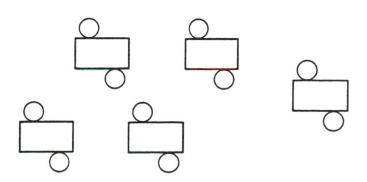

7. **Breakout groupings:** If your classroom is large enough or if nearby space is available, place (in advance when feasible) tables and/or chairs to which subgroups can go for team-based learning activities. Keep the breakout settings as far from each other as possible so that teams do not disturb one another. But avoid placing breakout spaces so far from the classroom that the connection to it is difficult to maintain.

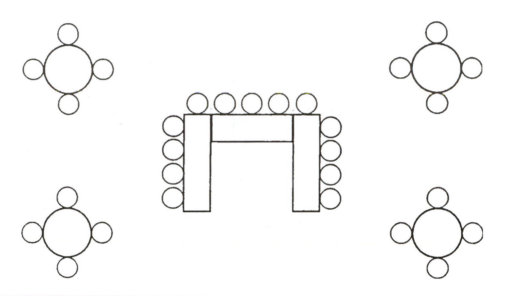

8. **Chevron arrangement:** A traditional classroom setup (rows of desks) does not promote active learning. When there are several students (30 or more) and only oblong tables are available, it is sometimes necessary to arrange students "classroom style." A repeated V or chevron arrangement creates less distance between people, better frontal visibility, and more ability to see other students than straight rows. In this arrangement, it's best to place aisles off-center.

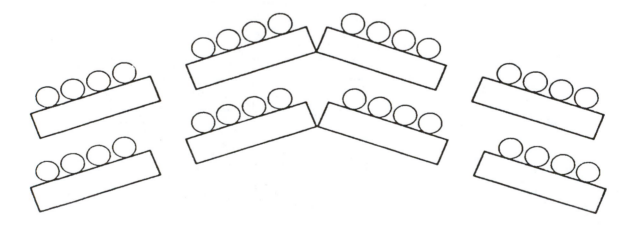

9. **Traditional classroom:** If there is no way to get around a series of straight rows of desks or tables and chairs, try grouping chairs in pairs to allow for the use of learning partners. Try to create an even number of rows and enough space between them so that pairs of students in the odd-numbered rows can turn their chairs around and create a quartet with the pair seated directly behind them in the next row.

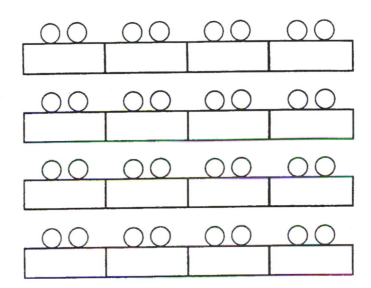

10. **Auditorium:** Although an auditorium provides a very limiting environment for active learning, there is still hope. If the seats are movable, place them in an arc to create greater closeness and student visibility.

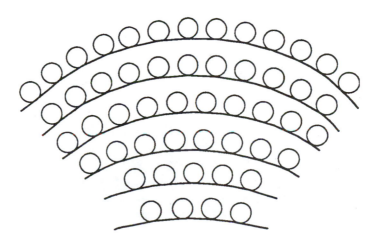

If the seats are fixed, ask students to seat themselves as close to the center as possible. Be assertive about this request; even consider cordoning off sections of the auditorium. Remember: No matter how big the auditorium and how large the audience, you can still pair up students and use active learning activities that involve partners.

Ten Methods to Get Participation at Any Time

Active learning cannot occur without student participation. There are various ways to structure discussion and obtain responses from students at any time during a class. Some are especially suitable when time is limited or participation needs to be coaxed. You might also consider combining these methods—for example, using subdiscussion and then inviting a spokesperson from each group to serve on a panel.

1. **Open discussion:** Ask a question and open it up to the entire group without any further structuring. The straightforward quality of open discussion is appealing. If you are worried that the discussion might be too lengthy, say beforehand, "I'd like to ask four or five students to share . . ." To encourage students to raise their hands, ask, "How many of you have a response to my question?" Then, call on a student with his or her hand raised.

2. **Response cards:** Pass out index cards and request anonymous answers to your questions. Have the index cards passed around the group or otherwise distributed. Use response cards to save time or to provide anonymity for personally threatening self-disclosures. The need to state your answer concisely on a card is another advantage.

3. **Polling:** Design a short survey that is filled out and tallied on the spot, or poll students verbally. Use pollying to obtain data quickly and in a quantifiable form. If you use a written survey, try to feed back the results to students as quickly as possible. If you use a verbal survey, ask for a show of hands or invite students to hold up answer cards.

4. **Subgroup discussion:** Break students into subgroups of three or more to share (and record) information. Use subgroup discussion when you have sufficient time to process questions and issues. This is one of the key methods for obtaining everyone's participation.

5. **Learning partners:** Have students work on tasks or discuss key questions with the student seated next to them. Use learning partners when you want to involve everybody but don't have enough time for small-group discussion. A pair is a good group configuration for developing a supportive relationship and/or for working on complex activities that would not lend themselves to large-group configurations.

6. **Whips:** Go around the group and obtain short responses to key questions. Use whips when you want to obtain something quickly from each student. Sentence stems (e.g., "One change I would make in the United States is . . .") are useful in conducting whips. Invite students to "pass" whenever they wish. To avoid repetition, ask each student for a new contribution to the process.

7. **Panels:** Invite a small number of students to present their views in front of the entire class. An informal panel can be created by asking for the views of a designated number of students who remain in their seats. Use panels when time permits to have a focused serious response to your questions. Rotate panelists to increase participation.

8. **Fishbowl:** Ask a portion of the class to form a discussion circle, and have the remaining students form a listening circle around them. Bring new groups into the inner circle to continue the discussion. Use fishbowls to help bring focus to large-group discussions. Though time consuming, this is the best method for combining the virtues of large- and small-group discussion. As a variation on concentric circles, have students remain seated at a table and invite different tables or parts of a table to be the discussants as the others listen.

9. **Games:** Use a fun exercise or a quiz game to elicit students' ideas, knowledge, or skill. TV game shows such as Family Feud or Jeopardy can be used as the basis of a game that elicits participation. Use games to spark energy and involvement. Games are also helpful to make dramatic points that students seldom forget.

10. **Calling on the next speaker:** Ask students to raise their hands when they want to share their views, and request that the present speaker call on the next speaker (rather than the teacher performing this role). Use this technique when you are sure there is a lot of interest in the discussion or activity and you wish to promote student interaction.

Ten Assignments to Give Learning Partners

Although we have just looked at ten ways to obtain student participation, the use of learning partners deserves special notice. One of the most effective and efficient ways to promote active learning is to divide a class into pairs and compose learning partnerships. It's hard to get left out in a pair. It's also hard to hide in one. Learning partnerships can be short or long term. Learning partners can undertake a wide variety of quick tasks or more time-consuming assignments, such as those in the following list.

1. **Discuss** a short written document together.

2. **Interview** each other concerning partner's reactions to an assigned reading, a lecture, a video, or any other educational activity.

3. **Critique** or edit each other's written work.

4. **Question** your partner about an assigned reading.

5. **Recap** a lesson or class session together.

6. **Develop** questions together to ask the teacher.

7. **Analyze** a case problem, exercise, or experiment together.

8. **Test** each other.

9. **Respond** to a question posed by the teacher.

10. **Compare** notes taken in class.

Ten Questions to Obtain Student Expectations

An active learning environment is a place where students' needs, expectations, and concerns influence the teacher's instructional plans. You can vary the questions you ask to find out from students what their goals are. Some may be especially appropriate to your situation. You can obtain answers through the ten methods to obtain participation that were described earlier.

1. What questions about (subject matter of class) do you come with?

2. What information or skills do you want to get from this class?

3. What information or skills don't you need or don't you want?

4. What do you want to take away from this class? Name one thing.

5. What are your hopes for this class? What are your concerns?

6. Do the class objectives match what you need?

7. What knowledge or skills do you feel you *need* to have? Which ones would be nice to have?

8. What are your expectations about this class?

9. Why did you choose this class (if the class is elective)? Why did you come?

10. What have you gotten from previous classes on this topic?

Ten Suggestions to Improve a Lecture

Lecturing is one of the most time-honored teaching methods, but does it have a place in an active learning environment? Used too often, lecturing will never lead to learning, but there are times when it can be effective. For that to happen, a teacher should build inter-

est first, maximize understanding and retention, involve students during the lecture, and reinforce what has been presented. Here are several options to do just that.

BUILDING INTEREST

1. **Lead-off story or interesting visual:** Provide a relevant anecdote, fictional story, cartoon, or graphic that captures the students' attention to what you are about to teach.

2. **Initial case problem:** Present a problem around which the lecture will be structured.

3. **Test question:** Ask students a question (even if they have little prior knowledge) so they will be motivated to listen to your lecture for the answer.

MAXIMIZING UNDERSTANDING AND RETENTION

4. **Headlines:** Reduce the major points in the lecture to key words that act as verbal subheadings or memory aids.

5. **Examples and analogies:** Provide real-life illustrations of the ideas in the lecture and, if possible, create a comparison between your material and the knowledge and experience students already have.

6. **Visual backup:** Use flip charts, transparencies, brief handouts, and demonstrations that enable students to see as well as hear what you are saying.

INVOLVING STUDENTS DURING THE LECTURE

7. **Spot challenges:** Interrupt the lecture periodically and challenge students to give examples of the concepts presented so far or to answer spot quiz questions.

8. **Illuminating exercises:** Throughout the presentation, intersperse brief activities that illuminate the points you are making.

REINFORCING THE LECTURE

9. **Application problem:** Pose a problem or question for students to solve based on the information given in the lecture.

10. **Student review:** Ask students to review the contents of the lecture with each other, or give them a self-scoring review test.

Ten Strategies to Form Learning Groups

Small-group work is a significant part of active learning. It's important to form groups quickly and efficiently and, at the same time, to vary the composition and sometimes the size of the groups throughout the class. The following options are interesting alternatives to letting students choose their own groups or counting off up to a number you have designated.

1. **Grouping cards:** Determine how many students are in the class and how many different groupings you want throughout the session. For example, in a class of twenty, one activity may call for four groups of five; another for five groups of four; still another for six groups of three with two observers. Code these groups using colored dots (red, blue, green, and yellow for four groups), decorative stickers (five different stickers on a common theme for five groups—for example, lions, monkeys, tigers, giraffes, elephants), and a number (1 through 6 for six groups). Randomly place a number, colored dot, and sticker on a card for each student and include the card in the student's materials. When you are ready to form your groups, identify the code you are using and direct the students to join their group in a designated place. Students will be able to move quickly to their groups, saving time and eliminating confusion. To make the process even more efficient, you may want to post signs indicating group meeting areas.

2. **Puzzles:** Purchase children's jigsaw puzzles or create your own by cutting out pictures from magazines; pasting them on cardboard; and cutting them into the desired shape, size, and number. Select the number of puzzles according to the number of groups you want to create. Separate the puzzles, mix up the pieces, and give each

student a puzzle piece. When you are ready to form your groups, instruct students to locate those with the other pieces needed to complete a puzzle.

3. **Finding famous fictional friends and families:** Create a list of famous fictional family members or friends in groups of three or four (e.g., Peter Pan, Tinker Bell, Captain Hook, Wendy; Alice, Cheshire Cat, Queen of Hearts, Mad Hatter; Superman, Lois Lane, Jimmy Olsen, Clark Kent). Choose the same number of fictional characters as there are students. Write the fictional names on index cards, one on each card, to create a family group of cards. Shuffle the cards and give each student a card with a fictional name. When you are ready to form groups, ask the students to find the other members of their "family." Once the famous group is complete, they can find a spot to congregate.

4. **Name tags:** Use name tags of different shapes and/or colors to designate different groupings.

5. **Birthdays:** Ask students to line up by birthdays, then break into the number of groups you need for a particular activity. In large classes, form groups by birth months. For example, 60 students can be divided into three groups of roughly equal size by composing groups of those born in (1) January, February, March, and April; (2) May, June, July, and August; and (3) September, October, November, and December.

6. **Playing cards:** Use a deck of playing cards to designate groups. For example, use jacks, queens, kings, and aces to create four groups of four, and add additional number cards depending on the number of students. Shuffle the cards and deal one to each student. Then direct students to locate others of their kind to form a group.

7. **Draw numbers:** Determine the number and size of the groups you want to create, put numbers on individual slips of paper, and place them in a box. Students draw a number from the box to indicate the group to which they belong. For example, if you want four groups of four, you would have sixteen slips of paper with four each of the numbers 1 through 4.

8. **Candy flavors:** Give students each a wrapped piece of sugarless hard candy of various flavors to indicate groupings. For example, your four groups might be lemon, butterscotch, cherry, and mint.

9. **Choose like items:** Select toys on a common theme and use them to indicate groups. For example, you might choose transportation and use cars, airplanes, boats, trains. Each student would "draw" a toy from a box and locate others with the same toy to form a group.

10. **Student materials:** You can code student learning materials using colored paper clips, colored handouts, or stickers on folders to predetermine groupings.

Ten Alternatives in Selecting Group Leaders and Filling Other Jobs

*One way to facilitate active learning in small groups is to assign jobs to some of the group members such as **leader, facilitator, timekeeper, recorder, spokesperson, process observer,** or **materials manager.** Often, you can simply ask for volunteers to assume some of these responsibilities. But sometimes it's fun and efficient to use a creative selection strategy.*

1. **Alphabetical assignment:** Identify the jobs needed and assign them in alphabetical order by first name. In a long-term group, rotate jobs using this order.

2. **Birthday assignment:** Make assignments in chronological order by students' birthdays (in the calendar year). In a long-term group, rotate jobs using this order.

3. **Number lottery:** Ask group members to count off. Place the numbers held by group members in a hat and pick the person for each job.

4. **Color lottery:** Select a color for each assignment. The person who is wearing something with a certain color receives that assignment.

5. **Clothing article:** Assign responsibilities by selecting corresponding articles of clothing, such as *eyeglasses, silver jewelry,* a *sweater,* or *brown shoes.*

6. **Voting:** Ask group members to vote on the job recipient. One popular method is to signal members to point to the person for whom they are voting. The person with the most fingers pointing at him or her gets the job.

7. **Random assignment:** Ask each member to calculate and reveal the sum of the last four digits of his or her home phone number (e.g., 9999 equals 36). Then announce a number from 1 to 36. The person in the group whose sum comes closest to that number will be the person assigned to the job.

8. **Pet lovers:** Assign a designated job to the person with the greatest number of pets.

9. **Family size:** Assign a designed job to the person with the most (or fewest) siblings.

10. **Door prize:** Prior to class, place a sticker in such a way as to identify one member per group. Methods include a sticker on a name tag, on a seat or desk, on one of the instructional handouts, and the like. The person receiving the sticker gets the "prize" of a specific group job. To award more than one job, use stickers of different colors.

Ten Tips When Facilitating Discussion

Class discussion plays a vital role in active learning. Hearing a wide variety of views challenges students' thinking. Your role during a group discussion is to facilitate the flow of comments from students. Although it is not necessary to interject after each student speaks, periodically assisting the group with their contributions can be helpful. Here is a ten point facilitation menu to use as you lead group discussions.

1. **Paraphrase** what someone has said so that the student feels understood and the other students can hear a concise summary of what's been said at greater length:

   So, what you're saying is that you have to be very careful about the words you use because a particular person might be offended by them.

2. **Check** your understanding against the words of a student or ask a student to clarify what he or she is saying:

    Are you saying that this political correctness has gone too far? I'm not sure that I understand exactly what you meant. Could you please run it by us again?

3. **Compliment** an interesting or insightful comment:

    That's a good point. I'm glad that you brought that to our attention.

4. **Elaborate** on a student's contribution to the discussion with examples, or suggest a new way to view the problem:

    Your comments provide an interesting point from the minority perspective. We could also consider how the majority would view the same situation.

5. **Energize** a discussion by quickening the pace, using humor, or, if necessary, prodding the group for more contributions.

    Oh my, we have lots of quiet people in this class! Here's a challenge for you. For the next two minutes, let's see how many words can you think of that are no longer politically acceptable.

6. **Disagree** (gently) with a student's comments to stimulate further discussion.

    I can see where you are coming from, but I'm not sure that what you are describing is always the case. Has anyone else had an experience that is different than Jim's?

7. **Mediate** differences of opinion between students, and relieve any tensions that may be brewing.

    I think that Susan and Mary are not really disagreeing with each other but are just bringing out two different sides of this issue.

8. **Pull together** ideas, showing their relationship to each other.

    As you can see from Dan's and Jean's comments, the words we use can offend people. Both of them have given us an example of how they feel excluded by gender-bound words.

9. **Change** the group process by altering the method for obtaining participation or moving the group to a stage of evaluating ideas that have been placed before the group.

Let's break into smaller groups and see if you can come up with some criteria for establishing gender-sensitive word usage.

10. **Summarize** (and record, if desired) the major views of the group.

     I have noted three major ideas that have come from the group's discussion as to when words are harmful: (1) They exclude some people. (2) They insult some people. (3) They are determined only by the majority culture.

Ten Steps When Facilitating Experiential Activities

Experiential activities really help to make learning active. Such activities typically involve role playing, games, simulations, visualization, and problem-solving tasks. It's often far better for students to experience something rather than hear it talked about. When facilitating experiential activities, here are ten steps to consider.

1. **Explain your objectives.** Students like to know what is going to happen and why.

2. **Sell the benefits.** Explain why you were doing the activity and share how the activity connects with the other activities before it.

3. **Speak slowly when giving directions.** You might also provide visual backup. Make sure the instructions are understandable.

4. **Demonstrate the activity if the directions are complicated.** Let the students see it in action before they do it.

5. **Divide students into subgroups before giving further directions.** If you don't, students may forget the instructions while the groups are being formed.

6. **Inform students how much time they have.** State the time allotted for the entire activity, and then announce periodically how much time remains.

7. **Keep the activity moving.** Don't slow things down by endlessly recording student contributions on flip charts or blackboards, and don't let a discussion drag on too long.

8. **Challenge the students.** There is more energy when activities create a moderate level of tension. If tasks are a snap, students will get lethargic.

9. **Always discuss the activity.** When an activity has concluded, invite students to "process" the feelings that the activity elicited and share the insights and learnings it contained.

10. **Carefully structure the first processing experiences.** Guide the discussion and ask only a few questions. If students are in sub-groups, ask them to take a brief turn sharing their responses.

Ten Options for Role Playing

Role playing is an especially useful experiential learning method. It can be used to spark a discussion, to reenact an event, to practice skills, or to exprience how certain phenomena feel. To be successful when conducting role playing, however, it helps to know different ways to set it up (scripting) and lead it (formatting).

SCRIPTING

1. **Free form:** Students can be given a general scenario and asked to fill in the details themselves.

2. **Prescribed:** Students can be given well-prepared instructions that state the facts about the roles they are portraying and how they are to behave.

3. **Semiprescribed:** Students can be given extensive background information about the situation and the characters to be portrayed, but not told how to handle the situation.

4. **Replay life:** Students can portray themselves in an actual situation they have faced.

5. **Dramatic reading:** Students can be given a previously prepared script to act out.

FORMATTING

6. **Simultaneous:** All students can be formed into pairs for a two-person drama, trios for a three-person drama, and so on, and can simultaneously undertake their role plays.

7. **Stage front:** One or more students can role-play in front of the group and the rest of the group can serve as feedback observers.

8. **Rotational:** Actors in front of the group can be rotated, usually by interrupting the role play in progress and substituting for one or more of the actors.

9. **Different actors:** More than one actor can be recruited to role-play the same situation in its entirety. This allows the group to observe more than one style.

10. **Repeated:** The role play can be practiced a second time.

Ten Time Savers When Active Learning Takes Time

Whatever methods you use, active learning takes time. Therefore, it is crucial that no time is wasted. Many teachers, however, lose control of time by allowing a number of time wasters to occur. Here are things you can do to save time.

1. **Start on time.** This act sends a message to latecomers that you're serious. If all of the students are not yet in the room, you can begin the class with a discussion or filler activity for which complete attendance is not necessary.

2. **Give clear instructions.** Don't start an activity when students are confused about what to do. If the directions are complicated, put them in writing.

3. **Prepare visual information ahead of time.** Don't write lecture points on flip charts or the blackboard while students watch. Have points prerecorded. Also, decide if recording student input is really necessary. If so, don't record all the words coming from class discussion. Use "headlines" to capture what students are saying.

4. **Move distribution of handouts quickly.** Put handouts in prepared stapled packets; distribute packets to key areas of the classroom so that several people can help with their distribution.

5. **Expedite subgroup reporting.** Ask subgroups to list their ideas on flip chart paper and post their lists on the walls of the classroom

so that all groups' work can be viewed and discussed at the same time. Or, going from group to group, have each one report only one item at a time so that everyone can listen for possible overlap. Subgroups should not repeat what has already been said.

6. **Don't let discussions drag on.** Express the need to move on, but, during a subsequent discussion, be sure to call on those who were cut off. Or begin a discussion by stating a time limit and suggesting how many contributions time will permit.

7. **Swiftly obtain volunteers.** Don't wait endlessly for volunteers to emerge. Recruit volunteers before class starts or restarts after a break; consistently call on individual students when there are no immediate volunteers.

8. **Be prepared for tired or lethargic groups.** Provide a list of ideas, questions, or even answers, and ask students to select ones they agree with; frequently, your list will trigger thoughts and issues from students.

9. **Quicken the pace of activities from time to time.** Often, putting students under time pressure energizes them and makes them more productive.

10. **Get the class's prompt attention.** Use a variety of cues or attention-getting devises to inform the class that you are ready to reconvene them after small-group activity.

Ten Interventions When Students Get Out of Hand

Using active learning techniques tends to minimize the classroom management problems that often plague teachers who rely too heavily on lecture and full-group discussion. If difficulties such as monopolizing, distracting, and withdrawing behaviors still occur, here are some interventions you can use. Some work well with individual students; others work with the entire class.

1. **Signal nonverbally.** Make eye contact with students or move closer to them when they hold private conversations, start to fall asleep,

or hide from participation. Press your fingers together (unobtrusively) to signal wordy student to finish what they are saying. Make a "T" sign with your fingers to stop unwanted behavior.

2. **Listen actively.** When students monopolize discussion, go off on a tangent, or argue with you, interject with a summary of their views and then ask others to speak. Or you can acknowledge the value of their viewpoints or invite them to discuss their views with you during a break.

3. **Get your ducks in a row.** When the same students always speak up in class while others hold back, pose a question or problem and then ask how many people have a response to it. You should see new hands go up. Call on one of them. The same technique might work when trying to obtain volunteers for role playing.

4. **Invoke participation rules.** From time to time, tell students that you would like to use rules such as these:

   • No laughing during role playing.

   • Only students who have not spoken as yet can participate.

   • Build on each other's ideas.

   • Speak for yourself, not for others.

5. **Use good-natured humor.** One way to deflect difficult behavior is to use humor with students. Be careful, however, not be sarcastic or patronizing. Gently protest the harrassment (e.g., "Enough, enough for one day!"). Humorously, put yourself down instead of the students (e.g., "I guess I deserved this.")

6. **Connect on a personal level.** Whether the problem students are hostile or withdrawn, make a point of getting to know them during breaks. It's unlikely that students will continue to give you a hard time or remain distant if you've taken an interest in them.

7. **Change the method of participation.** Sometimes you can control the damage done by difficult students by inserting new formats such as using pairs or small groups rather than full-class activities.

8. **Ignore mildly negative behaviors.** Pay little or no attention to behaviors that are small nuisances. Carry on with the class and see if they go away.

9. **Discuss very negative behaviors in private.** You must call a stop to behaviors you find detrimental to learning. Firmly request, in private, a change in behavior of those students who are disruptive. If the entire class is involved, stop the lesson and explain clearly what you need from students to conduct the class effectively.

10. **Don't take personally the difficulties you encounter.** Remember that many problem behaviors have nothing to do with you. They are due to personal fears and needs or displaced anger toward someone else. See if you can pick up cues when this is the case and ask whether students can put aside the conditions affecting their positive involvement in the class.

References

Bruner, J. *Toward a Theory of Instruction.* Cambridge, MA: Harvard University Press, 1966.

Grinder, M. *Riding the Information Conveyor Belt.* Portland, OR: Metamorphus Press, 1991.

Holt, J. *How Children Learn.* New York: Pitman, 1967.

Johnson, D. W., Johnson, R. T., & Smith, K. A. *Active Learning: Cooperation in the College Classroom.* Edina, MN: Interaction Book Company, 1991.

Maslow, A. *Toward a Psychology of Being.* New York: Litton Educational Publishing, 1968.

McKeachie, W. *Teaching Tips: A Guidebook for the Beginning College Teacher.* Boston: D. C. Heath, 1986.

Pike, R. *Creative Training Techniques Handbook.* Minneapolis, MN: Lakewood Books, 1989.

Pollio, H. R. *What Students Think About and Do in College Lecture Classes.* Teaching–Learning Issues No. 53. Knoxville: Learning Research Center, University of Tennessee, 1984.

Rickard, H., Rogers, R., Ellis, N., & Beidleman, W. "Some Retention, But Not Enough." In *Teaching of Psychology,* 1988, *15,* 151–152.

Ruhl, K., Hughes, C., & Schloss, P. "Using the Pause Procedure to Enhance Lecture Recall." In *Teacher Education and Special Education,* 1987, *10*(1), 14–18.

Schroeder, C. "New Students—New Learning Styles." *Change,* September–October 1993, 21–26.

2

How to Get Students Active from the Start

As you begin any class, it is crucial to get students active from the start. If you don't, you run the risk that passivity will set in much like cement that has had time to dry. Structure opening activities that get students to become acquainted, move about, engage their minds, and hook their interest in the subject matter. These experiences can be considered the "appetizers" to the full meal—they give students a taste of what is to follow. Although some teachers choose to begin a course merely with a short introduction, adding at least one opening exercise to your teaching plans is a first step that has many benefits. Let us explore why.

STARTING GOALS

In the earliest moments of active learning, there are three important goals to accomplish. Their importance should not be overlooked even if the class lasts for only one session. These goals are as follows:

1. **Team building:** Help students to become acquainted with each other and create a spirit of cooperation and interdependence.
2. **On-the-spot assessment:** Learn about the attitudes, knowledge, and experience of the students.
3. **Immediate learning involvement:** Create initial interest in the subject matter.

All three goals, when accomplished, help to develop a learning environment that involves students, promotes their willingness to take part in active learning, and creates positive classroom norms. Taking anywhere from five minutes to as much as two hours for opening activities (depending on the overall length of your class) will be time well spent. Reintroducing these activities from time to time throughout a course of study also helps to renew team building, refine assessment, and rebuild interest in the subject matter.

In this chapter, we will examine 23 strategies for accomplishing these three goals. You should find several that will work for you. As you select opening strategies to use in your class, keep in mind the following considerations:

1. **Level of threat:** Is the class that you are teaching open to new ideas and activities, or do you anticipate hesitation and reservation from students in the beginning? Opening with a strategy that exposes students' lack of knowledge or skill can be risky: They may not be ready to reveal their limitations. Alternatively, a strategy that asks participants to comment on something familiar to them eases their involvement into the class.

2. **Appropriateness to student norms:** A class of adolescents or adults may be initially less accepting of playing games than would a group of fifth graders. Female students may feel more comfortable sharing their feelings in a self-disclosure exercise than male students. You are setting the stage for the entire class as you select an opening activity; consider your audience and plan appropriately.

3. **Relevance to the subject matter:** Unless you are interested in a simple exchange of names, the strategies you are about to read offer an excellent opportunity for students to begin learning course material. Alter a suggested icebreaker so that it reflects the material that you are planning to teach in your course. The closer the tie-in of your exercise to your subject matter, the easier transition you will be able to make to the major learning activities you have in store.

These considerations have relevance for every aspect of your course of instruction, yet are especially important in the opening stages. A successful opening sets the stage for a successful class. Likewise, an opening that seems threatening, silly, or unrelated to the rest of your course can create an awkward atmosphere that is difficult to overcome.

Team-Building Strategies

The first set of strategies helps students to get acquainted and reacquainted or to build team spirit with a group who already know one another. These strategies also promote an active learning environment by getting students to move physically, to share their opinions and feelings openly, and to accomplish something in which they can take pride. Many of these strategies are well known throughout the teaching profession. Some are my own original creations. All of them get students active from the start.

When you use these team-building strategies, try to relate them to the subject matter of your class. Also, experiment with strategies new to you and your students. In today's world, students are so accustomed to certain popular icebreakers that they may be turned off to them rather than turned on. They will welcome activities that are refreshingly different.

1
Trading Places

OVERVIEW

This strategy allows students to get acquainted, exchange opinions and consider new ideas, values, or solutions to problems. It's a great way to promote self-disclosure or an active exchange of viewpoints.

PROCEDURE

1. Give students one or more Post-it™ notes. [Decide whether the activity will work better by limiting the students to one contribution or several.]
2. Ask them to write on their note(s) one of the following:
    a. A *value* they hold
    b. An *experience* they have had recently
    c. A creative *idea* or solution to a problem you have posed
    d. A *question* they have about the subject matter of the class
    e. An *opinion* they hold about a topic of your choosing
    f. A *fact* about themselves or the subject matter of the class
3. Ask students to stick the note(s) on their clothing and circulate around the room reading each other's notes.
4. Next, have students mingle once again and negotiate a trade of Post-it notes with one another. The trade should be based on a desire to possess a particular value, experience, idea, question, opinion, or fact for a short period of time. Set the rule that all trades have to be two-way. Encourage students to make as many trades as they like.
5. Reconvene the class and ask students to share what trades they made and why. (e.g., "I traded for a note that Sally had, stating that she has traveled to Eastern Europe. I would really like to travel there because I have ancestors from Hungary and the Ukraine.")

VARIATIONS

1. Ask students to form subgroups rather than trade notes, and have them discuss the contents of their notes.
2. Have students post their notes in a public display (on a blackboard, flip chart, etc.) and discuss similarities and differences.

2
Who's in the Class?

OVERVIEW

This popular icebreaker is a scavenger hunt for classmates rather than for objects. The hunt can be designed in a number of ways and for a class of any size. It fosters team building and gets physical movement going right at the beginning of a class.

PROCEDURE

1. Devise 6 to 10 descriptive statements to complete the phrase: ***Find someone who . . .***

    Include statements that identify personal information and/or class content. Use some of these beginnings:

Find someone who . . .

likes/enjoys _____

knows what a _____ is

thinks that _____

is good at _____

has already _____

is motivated by _____

believes that _____

has recently read a book about _____

has experience with _____

dislikes _____

has previously learned _____

has a great idea for _____

owns a _____

wants or doesn't want _____

2. Distribute the statements to students and give the following instructions:

This activity is like a scavenger hunt, except that you are looking for people instead of objects. When I say "begin," circulate around the room looking for people who match these statements. You can use each person for only one statement, even if he or she matches more than one. When you have found a match, write down the person's first name.

3. When most students have finished, call a stop to the hunt and reconvene the full class.
4. You may want to offer a token prize to the person who finishes first. More important, survey the class about each item. Promote short discussions of some of the items that might stimulate interest in the class topic.

VARIATIONS

1. Avoid competition entirely by allowing enough time for everyone to complete the scavenger hunt (as far as possible).
2. Ask students to meet others and find out how many matches can be made with each person.

3

Group Résumé

OVERVIEW

Résumés typically describe an individual's accomplishments. A group résumé is a fun way to help students become acquainted or do some team building of a group whose members already know one another. This activity can be especially effective if the résumé is geared to the subject matter you are teaching.

PROCEDURE

1. Divide students into groups of 3 to 6 members.
2. Tell the class that it contains an incredible array of talents and experiences!
3. Suggest that one way to identify and brag about the class's resources is to compose a group résumé. (You may want to suggest an imaginary job or contract he class could be bidding for.)
4. Give the groups newsprint and markers to display their résumés. It should include any information that sells the group as a whole. Included can be data about:

   > Educational background; schools attended
   > Knowledge about the class content
   > Job experience
   > Positions held
   > Skills
   > Hobbies, talents, travel, family
   > Accomplishments

5. Invite each group to present its résumé and celebrate the total resources contained within the entire group. Here is a résumé that a group might develop in a business writing class:

Writers R Us
[Todd, Pat, Shawna, Eli]

OBJECTIVE

Desire experience with creating professional documents and editing skills

QUALIFICATIONS

- 8 years in the job market
- 4 years of college education
- Knowledge of:
    Subject/verb agreement
    Active and passive verbs
    Dangling participles
    Comma usage
    Capitalization
    Commonly misspelled or confused words
- Owners of 2 personal computers
- Familiarity with Word Perfect and Microsoft Word
- Hobbies include cooking, sunbathing, dancing, and shopping.

VARIATIONS

1. To expedite the activity, give out a preprepared résumé outline that specifies the information to be gathered.
2. Instead of having students compile a résumé, ask them to interview one another about categories you provide.

4
Predictions

OVERVIEW

This is a fascinating way to help students become acquainted with one another. It also is an interesting experiment in first impressions.

PROCEDURE

1. Form subgroups of 3 or 4 students (who are relative strangers to each other).
2. Tell students that their job is to predict how each person in their group would answer certain questions you have prepared for them. Here are some all-purpose possibilities:

   a. What type of music do you enjoy?
   b. What are some of your favorite leisure activities?
   c. How many hours do you usually sleep nightly?
   d. How many siblings do you have and where are you in the sibling order?
   e. Where did you grow up?
   f. What were you like as a younger child?
   g. Are your parents strict or lenient?
   h. What jobs have you had?

   Note: Other questions can be added or substituted depending on the students in your class.

3. Have subgroups begin by selecting one person as its first "subject." Urge group members to be as specific as possible in their predictions about that person. Tell them not to be afraid of bold guesses! As they guess, ask the "subject" to give no indication of the accuracy of the predictions attempted. When others finish their predictions about the "subject," the "subject" should then reveal the answer to each question about him or herself.
4. Have each group member take a turn as the focus person.

VARIATIONS

1. Create questions that require students to make predictions about each other's views and beliefs (rather than factual information.) For example, ask: "What's the most important quality a friend should have?"
2. Eliminate the predictions. Instead, invite students, one by one, to answer the questions immediately. Then, ask subgroup members to reveal what facts about each other "surprised" them (based on their first impressions).

5
TV Commercial

OVERVIEW

This is an excellent opener for students who already know each other. It can produce rapid team building.

PROCEDURE

1. Divide students into teams of no more than 6 members.
2. Ask teams to create a thirty-second television commercial that advertises the subject of the class—emphasizing, for example, its value to them (or to the world!), famous people associated with it, and so forth.
3. The commercial should contain a slogan (e.g., "Better Living through Chemistry") and visuals (e.g., well-known chemical products).
4. Explain that the general concept and an outline of the commercial is sufficient. But if a team wants to act out its commercial, that is fine, too.
5. Before each team begins planning its commercial, discuss the characteristics of some well-known current commercials to stimulate creativity (e.g., use of a well-known personality, humor, comparison to competition, sex appeal).
6. Ask each team to present its ideas. Praise everyone's creativity.

VARIATIONS

1. Have teams create print advertisements instead of TV commercials. Or, if possible, have them actually create commercials on videotape.
2. Invite teams to advertise their talents or their school rather than the subject matter of the class.

6

The Company You Keep

OVERVIEW

This activity introduces physical movement right from the start and helps students get acquainted. It moves rapidly and is a lot of fun.

PROCEDURE

1. Make a list of categories you think might be appropriate in a getting-acquainted activity for the class you are teaching. All-purpose categories include:

    *   Month of birthday
    *   People who like/don't like (identify a preference, such as poetry, role playing, science, or computers)
    *   Favorite (identify any item, such as book, song, or fast food restaurant)
    *   The hand with which you write
    *   The color of your shoes
    *   Agreement or disagreement with any statement of opinion on a current issue (e.g., "Health care insurance should be universal.")

    You can also use categories that relate directly to the subject matter you are teaching, such as:

    *   Favorite author
    *   People who agree/disagree that (identify an issue related to your class topic)
    *   People who know/don't know who or what (identify a person or concept related to your class topic) is

2. Clear some floor space so that students can move around freely.
3. Call out a category. Direct students to locate as quickly as possible all the people whom they would associate with given the category. For example, *right-handers* and *left-handers* would separate into two groups, or those who agree with a statement would separate from those who disagree. If the category contains more than two choices (e.g., the month of students' birthdays), ask students to congregate with those like them, thereby forming several groups.
4. When students have formed the appropriate clusters, ask them to shake hands with "the company they keep." Invite all to observe approximately how many people there are in different groups.
5. Proceed immediately to the next category. Keep the students moving from group to group as you announce new categories.

6. Reconvene the entire class. Discuss the diversity of students revealed by the exercise.

VARIATIONS

1. Ask students to locate someone who is different from them rather than the same. For example, you might ask students to find someone who has eyes of a different color than theirs. (Whenever there are not equal numbers of students in different categories, allow more than one person from one group to cluster with someone from another group.)
2. Invite students to suggest categories.

7
Really Getting Acquainted

OVERVIEW

Most getting-acquainted activities are limited opportunities to get to meet others. An alternative is to arrange an in-depth experience in which pairs of students can become really well acquainted.

PROCEDURE

1. Pair up students in any manner you desire. Criteria for pairing up students might include:

    - Two students who have never met before
    - Two students who have never worked together
    - Two students who come from a different field of study or background
    - Two students who have a different level of knowledge or exprience

2. Ask pairs that are formed to spend 30 to 60 minutes getting to know each other. Suggest that they go for a walk, have coffee or a soda together, or, if relevant, visit each other's home or dorm.
3. Supply some questions that students can use to interview each other.
4. When the entire class reconvenes, give pairs a task to do together that enables them to start learning about the subject matter of the class. (See "Ten Assignments to Give Learning Partners" page 18).
5. Consider the appropriateness of forming the pairs into long-term learning partnerships.

VARIATIONS

1. If possible, form trios or quartets instead of pairs.
2. Have students introduce their partners to the entire class.

8

Team Getaway

OVERVIEW

Often, active learning is enhanced by creating long-term learning teams who might study together, do projects, and engage in other cooperative learning activities. When this is in your plans, it helps to conduct some initial team-building activities to ensure a solid start. While there are many team-building activities to consider, the following is a favorite.

PROCEDURE

1. Provide each team with a stack of index cards (different sizes in each stack are best).
2. Challenge each team to be as effective a group as possible by constructing a three-dimensional model of a "getaway retreat" solely from the index cards. Folding and tearing the cards are permitted, but no other supplies can be used for the construction. Encourage teams to plan their retreat before they begin to construct it. Provide marking pens so that teams can draw on the cards and decorate the getaway as they see fit.
3. Allow at least 15 minutes for the construction. Do not rush or pressure the teams. It is important for each to have a successful experience.
4. When the constructions are finished, invite the class to take a tour of the getaway retreats. Visit each construction and request that team members show off their work and explain any intricacies of their house. Applaud each team's accomplishments. **Do not encourage competitive comparisons among the constructions.**

VARIATIONS

1. Ask the teams to build a team monument instead of a getaway retreat. Urge them to make the monument sturdy, high, and aesthetically pleasing.
2. Reconvene the teams and ask them to reflect on the experience by responding to this question: **What were some helpful and not so helpful actions we did as a team and individually when working together?**

9
Reconnecting

OVERVIEW

In any class that meets over time, it is sometimes helpful to spend a few minutes reconnecting with students after some time has elapsed between classes. This activity considers some ways to do this.

PROCEDURE

1. Welcome students back to the class. Explain that you think it might be valuable to spend a few minutes becoming reconnected before proceeding with today's class.
2. Pose one or more of the following questions to the students:

   - What do you remember about our last class? What stands out for you?
   - Have you read/thought out/done something that was stimulated by our last class?
   - What interesting experiences have you had between classes?
   - What's on your mind right now (e.g., a worry) that might interfere with your ability to give full attention to today's class?
   - How do you feel today? (It can be fun to use a metaphor, such as a "I feel like a bruised banana.")
   - (Create your own question.)

3. Obtain responses by using any one of several formats, such as subgroups or call-on-the-next-speaker. (See "Ten Methods to Get Participation at Any Time" on page 16.)
4. Segue to the current class topic.

VARIATIONS

1. Conduct a review of the last class instead.
2. Present two questions, concepts, or pieces of information covered in the previous class. Ask students to vote for the one they would most like you to review with the class. Review the winning question, concept, or information.

10
The Great Wind Blows

OVERVIEW

This is a fast-paced icebreaker that gets students moving and laughing. It's a good team builder and allows students to get to know each other.

PROCEDURE

1. Arrange a circle of chairs. Ask each student to sit in one of the chairs. There should be exactly enough chairs for all students.
2. Tell students that if they agree with your next statement, they should stand up and move to another chair.
3. Stand in the center of the circle and say: "My name is _____ and THE GREAT WIND BLOWS for everybody who . . ." Choose an ending that would likely apply to nearly everyone in the class, such as "likes chocolate ice cream."
4. At this point, everyone who likes chocolate ice cream gets up and runs to another empty chair. As the students move, make sure you occupy one of the empty seats. If you do, then one student will have no seat to occupy and will replace you as the person in the center.
5. Have the new person in the center finish the same incomplete sentence: "My name is _____ and THE GREAT WIND BLOWS for everybody who . . ." with a new ending. It can be humorous (e.g., "who sleeps with a night light") or serious (e.g., "who is worried about the federal deficit").
5. Play the game as often as it seems appropriate.

VARIATIONS

1. Provide an extensive list of endings that the students can use. Include material relevant to the subject matter of the class (e.g., "who prefers a Macintosh to a PC") or to the job or life experience of the students ("who finds taking tests stressful").
2. Have pairs of students in the center instead of just one. Invite them to jointly select an appropriate ending for the sentence.

11
Setting Class Ground Rules

OVERVIEW

This is a polling method that enables students to set their own rules for behavior. When students are part of this team-building process, they are more likely to support the norms that are established.

PROCEDURE

1. Obtain a small number of volunteers (relative to the size of the class) to serve as interviewers.
2. During a period of 10 to 15 minutes, have interviewers circulate throughout the class, making contact with as large a sample of people as time permits. Instruct them to ask class members the following question: "What behaviors do you think would be helpful or not helpful to occur in this class among students?" (Provide some example answers to guide responses.)
3. At the end of the allotted period, ask interviewers to report their findings back to the class. (If desired, list the findings on a flip chart or blackboard.)
4. Usually, it is sufficient simply to hear the collected expressions of students to establish a sense of the behavioral ground rules desired by the group. However, it is also possible to analyze the findings, looking for overlap and then consolidating the list.

VARIATIONS

1. Provide a list of several possible ground rules. Ask students to select three from the list. Tabulate the results. The following items might be suitable for your list:
   - Respect confidentiality.
   - Everyone participates when working in small groups or teams.
   - Observe the starting time of the class.
   - Get to know others different from yourself.
   - Let others finish what they are saying without being interrupted.
   - No putdowns or "cheap shots."
   - Speak for yourself.
   - Be brief and to the point when speaking.
   - Use gender-sensitive language.
   - Be prepared for class.

- Don't sit in the same seat for every session of the class.
- Agree to disagree.
- Give everyone a chance to speak.
- Build on each other's ideas before criticizing them.

2. As a class, brainstorm ground rules for class participation. Then use a procedure called *multivoting* to arrive at a final list. Multivoting is a method for reducing a list of items by one-half. Each student votes on as many items as he or she wants; the half of the items with the highest number of votes remains on the list. (The procedure can be repeated as often as desired; each vote reduces the list by one-half.)

On-the-Spot Assessment Strategies

The strategies that follow can be used in conjunction with team-building efforts or by themselves. They are designed to help you learn about your class while, at the same time, involving students right at the beginning. Some of the strategies allow you to assess specific things about your students, while others are versatile enough to give you an overall picture. On-the-spot assessment strategies are especially useful when you have not had the opportunity to learn about the characteristics of your students before the class starting date. They can also be used to corroborate information you have gathered prior to the class.

12
Assessment Search

OVERVIEW

This is an interesting way to assess your class on the spot and, at the same time, involve students right from the beginning in getting to know each other and working cooperatively.

PROCEDURE

1. Devise three or four questions to learn about your students. You may include questions about the following:

   - Their knowledge of the subject matter
   - Their attitudes about the subject matter
   - Experiences students have had relevant to the subject matter
   - Skills they have previously obtained
   - Their backgrounds
   - The needs or expectations they bring to this class

   Write the questions so that concrete answers are attainable. Avoid open-ended questions. For example, ask: "How many of the following _____ do you know?" rather than "What do you know about _____ ?"

2. Divide students into trios or quartets (depending on the number of questions you have created). Give each student one of each of the assessment questions. Ask him or her to interview the other students in the group and obtain (and record) answers to his or her assigned question.

3. Convene in subgroups all the students who have been assigned the same question. For example, if there are 18 students, arranged in trios, 6 of them will have been assigned the same question.

4. Ask each subgroup to pool their data and summarize it. Then ask each subgroup to report to the entire class what they have learned about one another.

VARIATIONS

1. Invite the students to devise their own questions.
2. Using the same questions, pair up students and have them interview each other. Poll the class afterwards to obtain results. (This variation is appropriate when dealing with a large class.)

13
Questions Students Have

OVERVIEW

This is a nonthreatening way to learn about the needs and expectations of students. It utilizes a technique that elicits participation through writing rather than speaking.

PROCEDURE

1. Hand out a blank index card to each student.
2. Ask each student to write down any question they have about the subject matter or the nature of the present class (names should be withheld). For example, a student might ask: "How is Algebra II different from Algebra I?" or "Will there be a term paper in this class?"
3. Have the cards passed around the group in a clockwise direction. As each card is passed on to the next person, he or she should read it and place a check mark on the card if it contains a question of concern for the reader as well.
4. When a student's card comes back to him or her, each person will have reviewed all of the "questions" of the group. At this point, identify the question that received the most votes (check marks). Respond to each of these questions by (a) giving an immediate but brief answer; (b) postponing the question to a later, more appropriate time in the course; or (c) noting that the course will not be able to address the question (promise a personal response, if possible).
5. Invite some students to share voluntarily their questions, even if they did not receive the most votes.
6. Collect all the cards. They may contain questions to which you might respond at a future class.

VARIATIONS

1. If the class is too large to take the time to pass all the cards around the group, break the class into subgroups and follow the same instructions. Or simply collect the cards without having them passed around and respond to a sample of them.
2. Instead of asking for questions on the index cards, ask students to write down their hopes and/or concerns about the class, the topics they would like you to cover, or the ground rules for class participation they would like to see observed.

14
Instant Assessment

OVERVIEW

This is a fun, nonthreatening strategy to get to know your students. You can use it to assess "instantly" students' background, experiences, attitudes, expectations, and concerns.

PROCEDURE

1. Create a set of "responder" cards for each student. These cards could contain the letters A, B, or C for multiple-choice questions, T or F for true/false questions, or numerical ratings such as 1–5. (If it is too time-consuming to make the cards in advance, have students create their own cards on the spot.)
2. Develop a set of statements to which students can respond with one of their cards. Here is an example for each type of responder card mentioned.

   - I am taking this course because . . .
     - **a.** it's required.
     - **b.** I am really interested in the subject.
     - **c.** it's supposed to be easy.
   - I am concerned that this course will be difficult for me. *True* or *False?*
   - I believe that this course will be useful to me in the future.

     1_____2_____3_____4_____5
     Strongly   Strongly
     Disagree   Agree

   You can create similar statements about your students' knowledge, attitudes, and experiences.
3. Read the first statement and ask students to answer by holding up the card of their choice.
4. Quickly assess the audience response. Invite a few students to share the reasons for their choices.
5. Continue with the remaining statements.

VARIATIONS

1. Instead of using cards, ask students to stand when their choice is announced.
2. Use a conventional show of hands, but add interest by encouraging students to raise both hands when they strongly agree with a response.

15

A Representative Sample

OVERVIEW

Sometimes a class is very large and it is impossible to quickly get a sense of who is in it. This procedure allows you to draw a representative sample of students from the entire class and get to know them by interviewing them publicly.

PROCEDURE

1. Explain that you would like to get to know everyone in the class, but the task would consume too much time.
2. Note that a quicker way to do this would be to create a small sample of students who represent some of the diversity in the class.
3. Mention some ways in which the students might be diverse. Ask for the first member of the "class representative sample" to volunteer. When that person raises his or her hand, ask a few questions to get to know the person and learn about his or her expectations, skills, experiences, background, opinions, and so forth.
4. Having heard the responses of the first volunteer, ask for a second volunteer who is different in some respects from the first volunteer.
5. Continue drawing new volunteers (you decide how many) who are different from those who have previously been interviewed.

VARIATIONS

1. Arrange a table and chairs suitable for a panel discussion. Invite each member of the sample to join the panel after he or she has been interviewed. When the panel is complete, ask questions of the panel as a whole about their expectations, skills, job experience, background, opinions, and the like, and/or invite the audience to ask questions as well.
2. Invite other students to meet with you at an out-of-classroom site and at a later date so that you can become acquainted. If possible, rotate meetings so that you meet everyone.

16
Class Concerns

OVERVIEW

Students usually hold some concerns about a class they are attending for the first time, especially if it features active learning. This activity allows these concerns to be expressed and discussed openly, yet in a safe manner.

PROCEDURE

1. Explain to students that they may have concerns about the class. These might include some of the following:

    - How difficult or time-consuming the work may be
    - How to participate freely and comfortably
    - How students will function in small learning groups
    - How available the teacher will be
    - Access to reading materials
    - The time schedule for the class

2. List these areas of concern on a board or flip chart. Obtain others from members of the class.
3. Devise any voting procedure that enables the class to select the top three or four concerns.
4. Form the class into three or four subgroups. Invite each group to elaborate on one of the concerns. Ask them to get specific about the concern.
5. Ask each group to summarize its discussion for the entire class. Obtain reactions.

VARIATIONS

1. Ask groups to think of some solutions either the students or teacher can undertake to ease the concern assigned to them.
2. Rather than end the activity with group reports, create a panel or fishbowl discussion (see "Ten Methods to Get Participation at Any Time," page 16).

Immediate Learning Involvement Strategies

Yet another way to get students active from the start is to use the following strategies. They are designed to plunge students immediately into the subject matter in order to build their interest, arouse their curiosity, and stimulate thinking. Students can't do anything if their brains—or, if you will, their "computers"—are not *on!* Many teachers make the mistake of teaching too early—before students are engaged and mentally ready. Using any of these strategies will correct that tendency.

17

Active Knowledge Sharing

OVERVIEW

This is a great way to draw students immediately into the subject matter of your course. You can also use it to assess the knowledge level of students while, at the same time, doing some team building. It works with any class and with any subject matter.

PROCEDURE

1. Provide a list of questions pertaining to the subject matter you will be teaching. You could include some or all of the following categories:

   - Words to define (e.g., "What does 'ambivalent' mean?")
   - Multiple-choice questions concerning facts or concepts (e.g., "A psychological test is valid if it (a) measures an attribute consistently over time and (b) measures what it purports to measure.")
   - People to identify (e.g., "Who is George Washington Carver?")
   - Questions concerning actions one could take in certain situations (e.g., "How do you register to vote?")
   - Incomplete sentences (e.g., "A _____ identifies the basic categories of tasks you can perform with a computer program.")

     For example, a history teacher could begin a course on the twentieth century by handing out the following quiz:
     a. What happened in the following years: 1918, 1929, 1945, 1963, 1984?
     b. Identify the following:
     Mussolini
     Chamberlain
     Trotsky
     Mao
     McCarthy (Joseph and Eugene)
     c. In your opinion, what is the most important event in the twentieth century?

2. Ask students to answer the questions as well as they can.
3. Then invite them to mill around the room, finding others who can answer questions they do not know how to answer. Encourage students to help each other.

4. Reconvene the full class and review the answers. Fill in answers unknown to any of the students. Use the information as a way to introduce topics of importance in the class.

VARIATIONS

1. Give each student an index card. Ask them to write down one piece of information they are sure is accurate concerning the subject matter of the class. Invite the students to mill around, sharing what they wrote on their cards. Encourage them to write down new information garnered from other students. As a full group, review the information collected.
2. Use opinion questions rather than factual ones, or mix factual questions with opinion questions.

18
Rotating Trio Exchange

OVERVIEW

This is an in-depth way for students to discuss issues with some (but usually not all) of their fellow classmates. The exchanges can be easily geared to the subject matter of any class.

PROCEDURE

1. Compose a variety of questions that help students begin discussion of the course content. Use questions with no right or wrong answers.

   For example, an English teacher might ask:
   * *What do you like about Shakespearean plays? What don't you like?*
   * *Why is Shakespeare considered one of the greatest playwrights of all time?*
   * *Pick any nineteenth- or twentieth-century playwright or filmwriter. How would you compare this person to Shakespeare?*

2. Divide students into trios. Arrange the trios in the room so that each trio can clearly see a trio to its right and one to its left. The overall configuration of the trios would be a circle or a square.

3. Give each trio an opening question (the same question for each trio) to discuss. Select the least challenging question you have devised to begin the trio exchange. Suggest that each person in the trio take a turn answering the question.

4. After a suitable period of discussion, ask the trios to assign a 0, 1, or 2 to each of its members. Direct the students with the number 1 to rotate one trio clockwise. Ask the students with the number 2 to rotate two trios clockwise. Ask the students with the number 0 to remain seated since they are permanent members of a trio site. Have them raise their hands high so that rotating students can find them. The result will be entirely new trios.

5. Start a new exchange with a new question. Increase the difficulty or "threat level" of the questions as you proceed to new rounds.

6. You can rotate trios as many times as you have questions to pose and discussion time to allot. Each time, use the same rotation procedure. For example, in a trio exchange of three rotations, each student will get to meet, in depth, six other students.

VARIATIONS

1. After each round of questions, quickly poll the full group about their responses before rotating students to new trios.
2. Use pairs or quartets instead of trios.

19
Go to Your Post

OVERVIEW

This is a well-known way to incorporate physical movement at the beginning of a class. This strategy is flexible enough to use for a variety of activities that are designed to stimulate initial interest in your subject matter.

PROCEDURE

1. Post signs around the classroom. You can use two signs to create a dichotomous choice or several signs to provide more options.
2. These signs can indicate a variety of preferences:

   - Topics or skills of interest to the students (e.g., word processing, databasing)
   - Questions about course content (e.g., "How does a turbo engine work?")
   - Different solutions to the same problem (e.g., capital punishment versus life sentence)
   - Different values (e.g., money, fame, family)
   - Different personal characteristics or styles (e.g., auditory, visual, kinesthetic)
   - Different authors or well-known people in a field (e.g., Thomas Jefferson, Franklin Delano Roosevelt, John F. Kennedy)
   - Different quotations, proverbs, or verses in a text (e.g., "Honor Your Mother and Father" versus "Question Authority")

3. Ask students to look at the signs and choose one. For example, some students might be more interested in word processing than databasing. Have them "sign up" for their preference by moving to the place in the classroom where their choice is posted.
4. Have the subgroups that have been created discuss among themselves why they have placed themselves by their sign. Ask a representative of each group to summarize their reasons.

VARIATIONS

1. Pair up students with different preferences and ask them to compare their views. Or create a discussion panel with representatives from each preference group.
2. Ask each preference group to make a presentation, create an advertisement, or pepare a skit advocating their preference.

20
Lightening the Learning Climate

OVERVIEW

A classroom can quickly achieve an informal, nonthreatening learning climate by inviting students to use creative humor about the subject matter at hand. This strategy does just that and, at the same time, gets students thinking.

PROCEDURE

1. Explain to students that you want to do a fun opening exercise with them before getting serious about the subject matter.
2. Divide them into subgroups. Give them an assignment that deliberately asks them to make fun of an important topic, concept, or issue in the course you are teaching.
3. Examples might be:

    *   *Government:* Outline the most oppressive or unworkable government imaginable.
    *   *Math:* Develop a list of the most ineffective ways to do mathematical calculations.
    *   *Health:* Create a diet totally lacking in nutrition.
    *   *Grammar:* Write a sentence containing as many grammatical errors as possible.
    *   *Engineering:* Design a bridge that is likely to fall.

4. Invite subgroups to present their "creations." Applaud the results.
5. Ask: "What did you learn about our subject matter from this exercise?"

VARIATIONS

1. The instructor can spoof the subject matter with a creation of his or her own making.
2. Create a multiple-choice pretest on the subject you are about to teach. Add humor to the choices given for each item. For each question, ask students to select the answer that they think could not possibly be the right one.

21
Exchanging Viewpoints

OVERVIEW

This activity can be used to stimulate immediate involvement in the subject matter of your class. It also alerts students to be careful listeners and open themselves to diverse viewpoints.

PROCEDURE

1. Give each student a name tag. Instruct students to write their names on their tags and wear them.
2. Ask students to pair off and introduce themselves to someone else. Then ask pairs to exchange their responses to a provocative question or statement that solicits their opinion about an issue concerning the subject matter you are teaching.

   - An example of a question is: "What limits should there be to foreign immigration?"
   - An example of a statement is: "The Bible is a divine book."

3. Call "time," and direct students to exchange name tags with their partners and then go on to meet another student. Ask students, instead of introducing themselves, to share the views of the person who was their previous partner (the person whose name tag they are now wearing).
4. Next, ask students to switch name tags again and find others to talk to, sharing only about the views of the persons whose name tags they are wearing.
5. Continue the process until most of the students have met. Then tell each student to retrieve his or her own name tag.

VARIATIONS

1. Use this name tag exchange process as a social icebreaker by instructing students to share background information about themselves rather than viewpoints about a provocative question or statement.
2. Eliminate an exchange of name tags. Instead, ask students to continue to meet new people, each time hearing their opinions about the question or statement given by you.

22

True or False?

OVERVIEW

This collaborative activity also stimulates instant involvement in the subject matter of your class. It promotes team building, knowledge sharing, and immediate learning.

PROCEDURE

1. Compose a list of statements relating to your subject matter, half of which are true and half of which are false. For example, the statement "Marijuana is addictive" is true, and the statement, "Alcohol is a stimulant" is false. Write each statement on a separate index card. Make sure there are as many cards as there are students in the class. (If there is an odd number of students, make up a card for yourself.)

2. Distribute one card to each student. Tell the class that their mission is to determine which cards are true and which are false. **Explain that they are free to use any method they want to accomplish the task.**

3. When the class is finished, have each card read and obtain the class's opinion about whether the statement is true or false. Allow for minority views!

4. Give feedback about each card, and note the ways in which the class worked together on the assignment.

5. Indicate that the positive team skills shown will be necessary throughout this class because of the active learning it will feature.

VARIATIONS

1. Before the activity begins, recruit some students as observers. Ask them to give feedback about the quality of teamwork that emerged.

2. Instead of factual statements, create a list of opinions and place each opinion on an index card. Distribute cards and ask students to attempt to reach a consensus about students' reactions to each opinion. Ask them to respect minority viewpoints.

23

Buying into the Course

OVERVIEW

This design provides a way for students to think about and acknowledge their individual responsibility for activity learning in this class.

PROCEDURE

1. Create copies of the following contract:

   I understand that in this class I will be learning about _____ (fill in subject matter). The objectives of this class are: (fill in your objectives).
   I am committed to these objectives and will strive to do the following:
   - *Use my time in this class to support these objectives through active participation.*
   - *Take responsibility for my own learning and not wait for someone else to motivate me.*
   - *Help others make the most of their learning by listening to what they have to say and offering constructive responses.*
   - *Think about, review, and apply what I have learned outside of class.*

   _____
   SIGNED   DATE

2. Share with students your pledge to do everything within your power to make this class an effective learning experience. Provide them with the objectives you intend to help them attain.
3. Distribute copies of the contract and ask them to read it. Explain that you cannot guarantee the attainment of the course objectives without their effort and commitment to active learning. Ask them to consider the seriousness of this collaboration by agreeing to sign such a written contract with themselves.
4. Provide time for discussion and reflection. Explain that students will keep their contracts. Leave it up to the students whether or not to sign the contracts.

VARIATIONS

1. Provide a written statement of your responsibilities in this class. Consider some of the following:

- Listen actively to what students have to say.
- Be supportive of students' attempts to take learning risks.
- Vary your teaching methods.
- Start and end class on time.
- Supply easy-to-read handouts or other instructional materials.
- Be open to student suggestions.
- Provide visual aids.

2. Ask students to state their expectations of your behavior as a teacher.

3

How to Help Students Acquire Knowledge, Skills, and Attitudes . . . Actively

If the strategies presented in the previous section were the "appetizers" for active learning, the ones you will soon be introduced to are the "entrées." Education at all levels is about acquiring *knowledge, skills,* and *attitudes.* Cognitive learning (knowledge) includes the gaining of information and concepts. It deals not only with comprehending the subject matter but also with analyzing and applying it to new situations. Behavioral learning (skills) includes the development of competence in students' ability to perform tasks, solve problems, and express themselves. Affective learning (attitudes) involves the examination and clarification of feelings and preferences. Students are involved in assessing themselves and their personal relationship to the subject matter. How knowledge, skills, and attitudes are acquired makes all the difference in the world. Will it be done passively or actively?

Active learning of information, skills, and attitudes occurs through a process of inquiry. Students are in a *searching* mode rather than a *reactive* one. That is, they are looking for answers to questions either posed *to* them or posed *by* them. They are seeking solutions to problems teachers have challenged them to solve. They are interested in obtaining information or skills to complete tasks assigned to them. And they are confronted with issues that compel them to examine what they believe and value. All this occurs when students are engaged in tasks and activities that gently push them to think, do, and feel. You can create these kinds of activities using the many strategies you will find in this section.

This section is divided into several parts:

FULL-CLASS LEARNING

This part deals with ways to make teacher-led instruction more interactive. You will find strategies for presenting information and ideas that engage students mentally.

STIMULATING DISCUSSION

This part explores ways to intensify dialogue and debate of key issues in your subject matter. You will find strategies that encourage active, widespread student participation.

PROMPTING QUESTIONS

This part examines ways to help students become willing to ask questions. You will find strategies that enable students to formulate pointed questions that clarify what you have taught them.

COLLABORATIVE LEARNING

This part presents ways to design learning tasks done in small groups of students. You will find strategies that foster student cooperation and interdependence.

PEER TEACHING

This part discusses ways to enable students to teach each other. You will find strategies that enable students to be co-collaborators in the teaching–learning process.

INDEPENDENT LEARNING

This part relates to learning activities performed by students individually and privately. You will find strategies to promote student responsibility for directing their own learning.

AFFECTIVE LEARNING

This part pertains to students to examining their feelings, values, and attitudes. You will find strategies to facilitate self-understanding and values clarification.

SKILL DEVELOPMENT

This part deals with learning and practicing skills—both technical and nontechnical. You will find strategies to expedite initial skill development and further practice.

Full-Class Learning

The strategies in this section are designed to enhance full-class instruction. As you will read, even lecture-based lesson presentations can be made active by utilizing a variety of techniques. You will also find ways to improve the viewing of videos and the appearance of guest presenters. Finally, you will find novel ways to teach difficult concepts and ideas so that student understanding is maximized.

24
Inquiring Minds Want to Know

OVERVIEW

This simple technique stimulates students' curiosity by encouraging speculation about a topic or question. Students are more likely to retain knowledge about previously uncovered subject matter if they are involved from the onset in a full-class learning experience.

PROCEDURE

1. Ask the class an intriguing question to stimulate curiosity about a subject you want to discuss. **The question should be one to which you expect that few students know the answer.**

    Here are a few examples of such questions:

    - *Everyday knowledge* ("Why do we have income tax?")
    - *How to* ("According to experts, what is the best way to preserve a mummy?")
    - *Definitions* ("What is a *black hole?*")
    - *Titles* ("What do you think Ibsen's play *A Doll's House* is about?")
    - *The ways things work* ("What makes a car go?")
    - *Outcomes* ("What do you think will be the ending of this plot?" "The solutions to this problem?")

2. Encourage speculation and wild guessing. Use phrases like "take a guess" or "take a stab."
3. Do not give feedback immediately. Accept all guesses. Build curiosity about the "real" answer.
4. Use the question as a lead into what you are about to teach. Include the answer to your question in your presentation. You should find that students are more attentive than usual.

VARIATIONS

1. Pair up students and ask them to collectively make a guess.
2. Instead of a question, tell students what you are about to teach them and why they should find it interesting. Try to spice up this introduction in the manner of "coming attractions" to a movie.

25

Listening Teams

OVERVIEW

This activity is a way to help students stay focused and alert during a lecture-based lesson. Listening teams create small groups responsible for clarifying the class material.

PROCEDURE

1. Divide the students into four teams, and give the teams these assignments:

Team	Role	Assignment
1	Questioners	After the lecture-based lesson, ask at least two questions about the material covered.
2	Agreers	After the lecture-based lesson, tell which points they agreed with (or found helpful) and explain why.
3	Nay-sayers	After the lecture-based lesson, comment on which point they disagreed with (or found unhelpful) and explain why.
4	Example givers	After the lecture-based lesson, give specific examples or applications of the material.

2. Present your lecture-based lesson. After it is over, give teams a few moments to complete their assignments.
3. Call on each team to question, to agree, and so forth. You should obtain more student participation than you ever imagined.

VARIATIONS

1. Create other roles. For example, ask a team to summarize the lecture-based lesson, or ask a team to create questions that test students' understanding of the material.
2. Give out questions in advance that will be answered in the lecture-based lesson. Challenge students to listen for the answers. The team that can answer the most questions wins.

26
Guided Note Taking

OVERVIEW

In this popular technique, you provide a prepared form that prompts students to take notes while you are teaching. Even a minimal gesture like this engages students more than if already completed instructional handouts are provided. There are a variety of methods to do guided note-taking. The simplest one involves filling in the blanks.

PROCEDURE

1. Prepare a handout that summarizes the major points of a lecture-based lesson you are about to give.
2. Instead of providing a complete text, leave portions of it blank.
3. Some ways to do this include:

   - Provide a series of terms and their definitions; leave either the terms or their definitions blank.

     _____: *a five-sided figure*

     Octagon: _____

   - Leave one or more of a series of points blank.

     The Roles of the Roman Senate
     - *Administer the laws and decrees enacted by the consuls.*

     - _____

     - *Receive foreign ambassadors.*

     - _____

   - Leave key words in a short paragraph blank.

     Today, managers often face problems such as low _____ , high _____ , and _____ quality of service. Traditional management solutions, often tend, like the _____ _____ , to generate _____ new problems for every one solved.

4. Distribute the handout to students. Explain that you have created the blanks in order to help them listen actively to your lecture-based lesson.

VARIATIONS

1. Provide a worksheet that provides the major subtopics of your material you are presenting. Leave plenty of space for note-taking. The result will look something like this:

    The Four Types of Unjust Societies According to Socrates
    Timocracy:

    Oligarchy:

    Democracy:

    Tyranny:

    [*Optional:* After the presentation, give students a second copy of the handouts with blanks. Challenge them to fill in the blanks without looking at their notes.]
2. Divide a lecture-based lesson into several sections. Ask students to listen intently while you are speaking but *not* to take notes. Instead, invite them to write down notes during the breaks in the lecture-based lesson.

27
Lecture Bingo

OVERVIEW

A lecture can be less boring and students will be more alert if you make it into this game. Here, key points are discussed while students play Bingo.

PROCEDURE

1. Create a lecture-based lesson with up to 9 key points.
2. Develop a Bingo card that contains these key points in a 3 × 3 grid. Place a different point in each of the boxes. If you have fewer than 9 key points, leave some boxes empty.
3. Create several additional Bingo cards with the same key points, *but* place the points in different boxes. The result should be that few, if any, Bingo cards are alike.
4. Distribute the Bingo cards to students. Also provide students with a strip of 9 self-sticking colored dots (approximately one-half or three-quarters inch in diameter). Instruct students that as your presentation proceeds from point to point, they should place a dot on their cards for each point that you discuss. (*Note:* Empty boxes cannot be covered with a dot.)
5. As students collect three vertical, horizontal, or diagonal dots in a row, they yell "Bingo!"
6. Complete the lecture-based lesson. Allow students to obtain Bingo as many times as they can.

VARIATIONS

1. Use key terms or names mentioned in your lecture-based lesson (rather than key points) as the basis for the Bingo cards. When the term or name is first mentioned, students can place a sticker in the appropriate box.
2. Create a 2 × 2 Bingo grid. Continue to have several key points, terms, or names discussed in your lecture-based lesson. Indicate only four of these on any one Bingo card. Try to make few, if any, cards alike by including different information on each card.

28

Synergetic Teaching

OVERVIEW

This method is a real change of pace. It allows students who have had different experiences learning the same material to compare notes.

PROCEDURE

1. Divide the class in half.
2. Sent one group to another room to read about the topic you are teaching. Make sure the reading material is well-formatted and easy to read.
3. During this time, give an oral, lecture-based lesson on the same material to the other half of the class.
4. Next, reverse learning experiences. Provide reading material on your topic for the group that has heard the lecture-based lesson and provide a lecture-based lesson for the reading group.
5. Pair up members for each group and have them recap what they have learned.

VARIATIONS

1. Ask half of the students to listen to a lecture-based lesson presentation with their eyes closed while the other half views visual information such as overhead transparencies accompanying the lecture-based lesson with their ears covered. After the lecture-based lesson is completed, ask the two groups to compare notes about what they have heard or seen.
2. Give one half of the class concrete examples of a concept or theory you want them to learn. Do not tell them about the concept or theory they illustrate. Present to the other half of the class the concept or theory without the examples. Pair up students from both groups and have them review the lesson together.

29
Guided Teaching

OVERVIEW

In this technique, the teacher asks one or more questions to tap the knowledge of the class or obtain their hypotheses or conclusions and then sorts them into categories. The guided teaching method is a nice break from straight lecturing and allows you to learn what students already know and understand before making instructional points. This method is especially useful when teaching abstract concepts.

PROCEDURE

1. Pose a question or a series of questions that taps students' thinking and existing knowledge. Utilize questions that have several possible answers, such as "How can you tell how intelligent someone is?"
2. Give students some time in pairs or subgroups to consider their responses.
3. Reconvene the entire class and record students' ideas. If possible, sort their responses into separate lists that correspond to different categories or concepts you are trying to teach. In the example question, you might list ideas such as "the ability to rebuild an engine" under the category *bodily-kinesthetic intelligence.*
4. Present the major learning points you want to teach. Have students figure out how their responses fit into these points. Note ideas that add to the learning points of your lesson.

VARIATIONS

1. Don't sort student responses into separate lists. Instead, create one continuous list and ask them to categorize their own ideas first before you compare them to the concepts you have in mind.
2. Begin the lesson with no preset categories you have in mind. See how the students and you together can sort ideas into useful categories.

30
Meet the Guest

OVERVIEW

This activity is an excellent way to involve guest speakers who don't have the time or expertise to prepare for a class session. At the same time, it gives students the opportunity to interact with a subject matter expert in a unique way and to take an active role in preparing for the guest speaker.

PROCEDURE

1. Invite a guest speaker(s) to address your class as the expert on the subject you are currently discussing. (*Example:* A local government official might visit a class on civics or government.)
2. Prepare the guest speaker by telling him or her that the session will be conducted like a press conference. In keeping with that format, the speaker is to prepare a few brief remarks or opening statement and then be prepared to answer questions from "the press."
3. Prior to the guest's appearance, prepare the students by discussing how a press conference is conducted, and then giving them an opportunity to formulate several questions to ask the speaker.

VARIATIONS

1. You may choose to have several guests at the same time and conduct roundtable discussions. Seat each guest at a table or in a circle of chairs to share information and experiences with a small group. The group members will have an opportunity to interact with the guest by asking questions in a more personal environment. Divide the class session into a series of rounds. Determine the length of each round depending on the time available and the number of guests. In general, 10 or 15 minutes for each round is appropriate. Direct each small group to move from one guest to the next as the rounds progress.
2. Invite some students from a previous class you taught to serve as visiting "guests."

31
Acting Out

OVERVIEW

Sometimes, no matter how clear a verbal or visual explanation is, some concepts and procedures don't sink in. One way to help develop a picture of the material is to ask some students to act out the concepts or walk through the procedures you are trying to get across.

PROCEDURE

1. Choose a concept (or a set of related concepts) or a procedure that can be illustrated by acting it out. Some examples include:

   - Sentence construction
   - Finding a common denominator
   - Corporeal (heart) circulation
   - Gothic architecture

2. Use any of the following methods:

   - Have some students come to the front of the room and ask them to simulate physically aspects of the concept or procedure.
   - Create large cards that name the parts of a procedure or concept. Give out cards to some students. Place students with cards in such a way that the cards are correctly sequenced.
   - Develop a role play in which students dramatize the material you are teaching.
   - Using volunteer students, walk through a step-by-step procedure.

3. Discuss the learning drama that you have created. Make whatever teaching points you want.

VARIATIONS

1. Videotape a group of students illustrating the concept or procedure and show it to the class.
2. Ask students to create a way to act out a concept or procedure without your guidance.

32
What's My Line?

OVERVIEW

This activity offers a fresh approach to helping students learn cognitive material. By adapting an old television game show, students have an opportunity to review material that has just been taught and test one another as a reinforcement to your lesson.

PROCEDURE

1. Divide your class into two or more teams.
2. Write on separate slips of paper any of the following:

   - I am: (supply a person)   e.g., *I am Karl Marx.*
   - I am: (supply an event)   e.g., *I am a "solar eclipse."*
   - I am: (supply a theory)   e.g., *I am "Darwinism."*
   - I am (supply a concept)   e.g., *I am "inflation."*
   - I am (supply a skill)   e.g., *I am "the Heimlich maneuver."*
   - I am: (supply a quotation)   e.g., *I am "to be or not to be."*
   - I am: (supply a formula)   e.g., *I am $e = mc^2$.*

3. Put these slips of paper in a box, and ask each team to choose one slip. The slip chosen reveals the identity of the mystery guest.
4. Give the teams five minutes to do the following tasks:

   - Choose a team member to be the "mystery guest."
   - Anticipate questions he or she will be asked and think how to respond.

5. Select the team that will present the first mystery guest.
6. Create a panel of students from other teams (by whatever method you choose).
7. Begin the game. Ask the mystery guest to reveal his or her category (person, event, etc.). The panelists take turns asking yes-or-no questions of the mystery guest until one of the panelists is able to identify the guest.
8. Invite the remaining teams to present their mystery guests. Create a new panel for each guest.

VARIATIONS

1. Allow each mystery guest to consult with his or her teammates if he or she is unsure how to answer the questions posed by the panelists.

2. The teacher may specify how he or she wants the mystery guest to act. For example, a guest might actually try to impersonate the famous person being portrayed.

33
Video Critic

OVERVIEW

Often, viewing educational videos is a passive affair. Students sit back in their seats, waiting to be entertained. This is an active way to engage students in watching a video.

PROCEDURE

1. Select a video that you want to show students.
2. Tell students, prior to watching the video, that you want them to critically review the video. Ask them to look at several factors, including:

   - Realism (of actors)
   - Relevance
   - Unforgettable moments
   - Organization of content
   - Applicability to their lives

3. Show the video.
4. Conduct a discussion you might call a "critic's corner."
5. (optional) Poll the class, using some kind of overall rating system, such as:

   - One to five stars
   - Thumbs up, thumbs down

VARIATIONS

1. Create a panel of video reviewers.
2. Show the video again. Sometimes critics change their minds when seeing something a second time.

Stimulating Class Discussion

All too often, a teacher tries to stimulate class discussion but is met with uncomfortable silence as students wonder who will dare to speak up first. Starting a discussion is no different from beginning a lecture-based lesson. You first have to build interest! The strategies that follow are sure-fire ways to stimulate discussion. Some will even create heated but manageable exchanges between students. All of them are designed so that *every* student is involved.

34
Active Debate

OVERVIEW

A debate can be a valuable method for promoting thinking and reflection, especially if students are expected to take a position that may be contrary to their own. This is a strategy for a debate that actively involves every student in the class—not just the debaters.

PROCEDURE

1. Develop a statement that takes a position with regard to a controversial issue relating to your subject matter (e.g., "The media creates news rather than reports it.")

2. Divide the class into two debating teams. Assign (arbitrarily) the "pro" position to one group and the "con" position to the other.

3. Next, create two to four subgroupings within each debating team. In a class of 24 students, for example, you might create three pro subgroups and three con subgroups, each containing four members. Ask each subgroup to develop arguments for its assigned position, or provide an extensive list of arguments they might discuss and select. At the end of their discussion, have the subgroup select a spokesperson.

4. Set up two to four chairs (depending on the number of subgroups created for each side) for the spokespersons of the pro side and, facing them, the same number of chairs for the spokespersons of the con side. Place the remaining students behind their debate team. For the preceding example, the arrangement will look like this:

x			x
x			x
x			x
x	pro	con	x
x	pro	con	x
x	pro	con	x
x			x
x			x
x			x

Begin the "debate" by having the spokespersons present their views. Refer to this process as "opening arguments."

5. After everyone has heard the opening arguments, stop the debate and reconvene the original subgroups. Ask the subgroups to strategize how to counter the opening arguments of the opposing side. Again, have each subgroup select a spokesperson, preferably a new person.

6. Resume the "debate." Have the spokespersons, seated across from each other, give "counterarguments." As the debate continues (be sure to alternate between the two sides), encourage other students to pass notes to their debaters with suggested arguments or rebuttals. Also, urge them to cheer or applaud the arguments of their debate team representatives.

7. When you think it appropriate, end the debate. Instead of declaring a winner, reconvene the entire class in a single circle. Be sure to integrate the class by having students sit next to people who were on opposite sides. Hold a classwide discussion on what students learned about the issue from the debate experience. Also, ask students to identify what they thought were the best arguments raised on both sides.

VARIATIONS

1. Add one or more empty chairs to the debate teams. Allow students to occupy these empty chairs whenever they want to join the debate.

2. Start the activity immediately with the opening arguments of the debate. Proceed with a conventional debate, but frequently rotate the debaters.

35
Town Meeting

OVERVIEW

This discussion format is well suited to large classes. By creating an atmosphere akin to a town meeting, the entire class can become involved in discussion.

PROCEDURE

1. Select an interesting topic or case problem concerning your subject matter. Briefly present the topic or problem as objectively as possible, giving background information and an overview of different viewpoints. If you wish, provide any documents that might illuminate the topic or problem.
2. Point out that you would like to obtain the class's own views on the matter. Instead of calling on students from the front of the room, explain that you will be following a format entitled "call on the next speaker." Whenever someone is finished speaking, that person should look around the room and call on somebody else who also wishes to speak (as indicated by a raised hand).
3. Urge students to keep their remarks brief so that many others can participate in the town meeting. Establish a time limit, if you wish, for the length of a speaker's turn. Direct students to call on someone who has not participated previously before choosing someone who already has taken a turn.
4. Continue the discussion as long as it seems of value.

VARIATIONS

1. Organize the meeting into a debate. Invite students to sit on different sides of the room, corresponding to their own positions on the controversy. Follow the call-on-the-next-speaker format, with the instruction that the next speaker must have an opposing point of view. Encourage students to move to a different side of the room if their views are swayed by the debate.
2. Begin the town meeting with a panel discussion. Have the panelists present their own views and then call on speakers from the audience.

36
Three-Stage Fishbowl Decision

OVERVIEW

A fishbowl is a discussion format in which a portion of the class forms a discussion circle and the remaining students form a listening circle around the discussion group (see "Ten Methods to Obtain Participation at Any Time," page 00). Following is one of the more interesting ways to set up a fishbowl discussion.

PROCEDURE

1. Devise three questions for discussion relevant to your subject matter. In a class on ecology, for example, the questions might be:

    *   *How is the environment being endangered?*
    *   *What steps can the government and private industry take to deal with the problem?*
    *   *What can we do personally?*

    Ideally, the questions should be interrelated, but that is not required. Decide in what order you would like the questions discussed.

2. Set up chairs in a fishbowl configuration (two concentric circles). Have the students count off by 1, 2, and 3. Ask the members of group 1 to occupy the discussion-circle seats and ask the members of groups 2 and 3 to sit in the outer-circle seats. Pose your first question for discussion. Allow up to 10 minutes for discussion. Invite one student to facilitate the discussion or act as the facilitator yourself.

3. Next, invite the members of group 2 to sit in the inner circle, replacing group 1 members who now sit in the outer circle. Ask the members of group 2 if they would like to make any brief comments about the first discussion, and then segue into the second discussion topic.

4. Follow the same procedure with members of group 3.

5. When all three questions have been discussed, reconvene the class as one discussion group. Ask them for their reflections about the entire discussion.

VARIATIONS

1. If it is not possible to have circles of chairs, have a rotating panel discussion instead. One-third of the class become panelists for each discussion question. The

panelists can sit in front of the classroom facing the remainder of the class. If you are using a U-shaped classroom arrangement or a conference table (see "Ten Layouts for Setting Up a Classroom," page 9), designate a side of the table as a panel group.

2. Use only one discussion question rather than three. Invite each subsequent group to respond to the discussion of the preceding group.

37
Expanding Panel

OVERVIEW

This activity is an excellent way to stimulate discussion and give students an opportunity to identify, explain, and clarify issues while securing active participation from the entire class.

PROCEDURE

1. Select an issue that will engage student interest. Present the issue so that students will be stimulated to discuss their viewpoints. Identify up to five questions for discussion.
2. Choose four to six people to serve as a panel discussion group. Arrange them in a semicircle at the front of the room.
3. Ask the rest of the class to surround the discussion group on three sides in a horseshoe arrangement.
4. Begin with a provocative opening question. Moderate a panel discussion with the core group while the observers take notes in preparation for their own discussion. For example, some points that might be raised in a discussion of the question "What are the pro's and con's of genetic engineering?" are:

   Pro
   Medical science has reached the stage where this is possible, so why deny it?
   Scientists will be able to eliminate some pain and suffering.
   Parents will be able to avoid having children with birth defects.

   Con
   Human beings should not tamper with God's plan.
   Genetic "freaks" might result.
   Parents should not be able to decide the type of children they want to have.

5. At the end of the designated discussion period, separate the entire class into small groups to continue the discussion of the remaining questions.

VARIATIONS

1. Reverse the sequence; begin with small group discussion and follow with a panel discussion.
2. Invite the students to generate the questions for discussion.

38
Point–Counterpoint

OVERVIEW

This activity is an excellent technique for stimulating discussion and gaining a deeper understanding of complex issues. The format is similar to a debate but is less formal and moves more quickly.

PROCEDURE

1. Select an issue that has two or more sides.
2. Divide the class into groups according to the number of positions you have stated, and ask each group to come up with arguments to support its side. Encourage them to work with seat partners or small cluster groups.
3. Reconvene the entire class, but ask members of each group to sit together with space between the subgroups.
4. Explain that any student can begin the debate. After that student has had an opportunity to present *one* argument in favor of his or her assigned position, allow a different argument or counterargument from other groups. Continue the discussion, moving quickly back and forth between or among the groups.
5. Conclude the activity by comparing the issues as you, the teacher, see them. Allow for follow-up reaction and discussion.

VARIATIONS

1. Instead of a group-on-group debate, pair up individual students from different groups and have them argue with each other. This can be done simultaneously, so that every student is engaged in the debate at the same time.
2. Line up the opposing groups so that they are facing each other. As one person concludes his or her argument, have that student toss an object (such as a ball or a bean bag) to a member of the opposing side. The person who catches the object must rebut the previous person's argument.

39
Reading Aloud

OVERVIEW

Surprisingly, reading a text out loud can help students to focus mentally, raise questions, and stimulate discussion. This strategy is much like a Bible study session. It has the effect of focusing attention and creating a cohesive group.

PROCEDURE

1. Choose a text that is sufficiently interesting to read aloud. Limit yourself to a selection of less than 500 words.
2. Introduce the text to the students. Highlight key points or issues to be raised.
3. Section off the text by paragraphs or some other means. Invite volunteers to read aloud different sections.
4. As the reading progresses, stop at several places to emphasize certain points, raise or entertain questions, or give examples. Allow brief discussions if students show an interest in a certain portion. Then proceed with examining what is in the text.

VARIATIONS

1. Do the reading yourself if you feel it will enhance the presentation of the text or you have concerns about the reading skills of students.
2. Have pairs read to each other, stopping for clarification and discussion as they see fit.

40
Trial by Jury

OVERVIEW

This technique utilizes a mock trial complete with witnesses, prosecutors, defenders, friends of the court, and more. It is a good method to spark "controversy learning"—learning by effectively arguing a viewpoint and challenging the opposite view.

PROCEDURE

1. Create an indictment that will help students see the different sides of an issue. Examples of "crimes" for which someone or something might be tried are: a literary character or real person with moral failings; a controversial book; an unproven theory; a value that does not have merit; and a faulty process, law, or institution.

2. Assign roles to students. Depending on the number of students, you could use all or some of these roles: defendant, defense attorney, defense witnesses, prosecuting attorney, prosecution witnesses, friends of the court, judge, jury member. Each role can be filled by one person or by a team. You could have any number in the jury.

3. Allow time for students to prepare. This could be a few minutes up to an hour, depending on the complexity of the issue.

4. Conduct the trial. Consider using these activities: opening arguments, case presented by the prosecutor and witnesses, friend of the court briefs, and closing arguments.

5. Conduct the jury deliberations. These should be done publicly, so everyone can hear how the evidence is being weighed. Non–jury members can be given an assignment to listen for various aspects of the case.

VARIATIONS

1. Extend the activity by staging a retrial.
2. Eliminate a trial by jury and substitute a trial by judge only.

Prompting Questions

"Are there any questions?" asks the teacher. All too often, what follows is stony silence. Some teachers may think the students aren't interested. Others may conclude that everything must be clear. Unfortunately, the truth is often that students aren't *ready* to ask questions. The strategies that follow will help you to change these dynamics. Students will be more challenged to compose questions because they have had a chance to think over the material.

41

Learning Starts with a Question

OVERVIEW

The process of learning something new is more effective if the learner is in an active, searching mode rather than a receptive one. One way to create this mode of active learning is to stimulate students to inquire into subject matter on their own, without prior explanation from the teacher. This simple strategy stimulates question asking, the key to learning.

PROCEDURE

1. Distribute to students an instructional handout of your own choosing. (You may use a page in a textbook instead of a handout.) Key to your choice of material is the need to stimulate questions on the part of the reader. A handout that provides broad information but lacks details or explanatory backup is ideal. An interesting chart or diagram that illustrates some knowledge is an good choice. A text that is open to interpretation is another good choice. The goal is to evoke curiosity.

2. Ask students to study the handout with a partner. Request that each pair make as much sense of the handout as possible and identify what they do not understand by marking up the document with questions next to information they do not understand. Encourage students to insert as many question marks as they wish. If time permits, form pairs into quartets and allow time for each pair to help the other.

   A physics teacher, for example, might distribute a diagram illustrating how potential energy converts to kinetic energy by showing a circus diver leaping from a 50-foot pole. Students work with a partner to review the illustration and determine questions (i.e., When exactly does the potential energy become kinetic energy? What is the basic difference between kinetic and potential energy?).

3. Reconvene the class and field students' questions. You are teaching through your answers to student questions rather than through a preset lesson. Or, if you wish, listen to the questions all together and then teach a preset lesson, making special efforts to respond to the questions students posed.

VARIATIONS

1. If you feel that students will be lost trying to study the material entirely on their own, provide some information that orients them or gives them the basic knowledge they need to be able to inquire on their own. Then proceed with the study groups.
2. Begin the procedure with individual study rather than partner study.

42
Planted Questions

OVERVIEW

This technique enables you to present information in response to questions that have been planted with selected students. Although you are, in effect, giving a well-prepared lesson, it appears to other students that you are merely conducting a question-and-answer session.

PROCEDURE

1. Choose questions that will guide your lesson. Write three to six questions and sequence them logically.
2. Write each of the questions on an index card, and write down the cue you will use to signal you want that question asked. Cues you might use include:
   - Scratching your nose
   - Taking off your eyeglasses
   - Snapping your fingers
   - Yawning

   The resulting instruction card might look like this:

DO NOT SHOW THIS CARD TO ANYONE.

When our break is over, I'm going to be discussing "Is intelligence inherited?" and then ask if there are any questions. When I scratch my nose, raise your hand and ask the following question:

Is there more than one kind of intelligence?

Do not read the question out loud. Memorize it or say it in your own words.

---

3. Prior to the lesson, select the students who will ask the questions. Give each an index card, and explain their cue. Make sure they do not reveal to anyone else that they are plants.
4. Open the question-and-answer session by announcing the topic and giving your first cue. Call on the first plant, answer the question, and then continue with the rest of the cues and questions.
5. Now, open the floor to new questions—not previously planted. You should see several hands go up.

VARIATIONS

1. Have the answers to the questions already on flip charts, overhead transparencies, or instructional handouts that you reveal as each question is answered. Dramatically reveal the answer as each question is given.
2. Give the planted questions to your most uninterested or hostile students.

43
Role Reversal Questions

OVERVIEW

Even if you ask students to think of questions during the heart of a lesson, not just at the end, you may get a lukewarm response when you ask, "Are there any questions?" With this technique, you reverse roles: You ask questions and the students try to respond.

PROCEDURE

1. Compose questions you would raise about some learning material **if you were a student.** Create questions that:

   - Seek to clarify difficult or complex material (e.g., "Would you explain again the way to _____?")
   - Compare the material to other information (e.g., "How is this different than _____?")
   - Challenge your own points of view (e.g., "Why is it necessary to do this? Wouldn't it lead to a lot of confusion?")
   - Request examples of the ideas being discussed (e.g., "Could you give me an example of _____?")
   - Test the applicability of the material (e.g., "How could I use this idea in real life?")

2. At the beginning of a question period, announce to the students that you are going to "be" them, and they collectively are going to "be" you. Proceed to ask your questions.
3. Be argumentative, humorous, or whatever else it takes to get them to jump into the fray and bombard you with answers.
4. Reversing roles a few times will keep your students on their toes and prompt them to ask questions on their own.

VARIATIONS

1. Instead of using this technique at the start of a question-and-answer session, revert to it when students have become complacent about questions.
2. Turn the event into a "media conference." You become the media, introducing yourself as "Chris from CNN" or the like, and press the class with questions that probe, attack, or mock the learning material in question.

Collaborative Learning

One of the best ways to promote active learning is to give learning assignments that are carried out in small groups of students. The peer support and diversity of viewpoints, knowledge, and skill help make collaborative learning a valuable part of your classroom learning climate. However, collaborative learning is not always effective. There may be unequal participation, poor communication, and confusion instead of real learning. The strategies that follow are designed to maximize the benefits of collaborative learning and to minimize the pitfalls.

44
Information Search

OVERVIEW

This method can be likened to an open-book test. Teams search for information (normally covered in a lecture-based lesson) that answers questions posed to them. This method is especially helpful in livening up dry material.

PROCEDURE

1. Create a group of questions that can be answered by searching for information that can be found in resource material you have made available for students. The resource material can include:

   - Handouts
   - Documents
   - A textbook
   - Reference guides
   - Computer-accessed information
   - Artifacts
   - "Hard" equipment (e.g., machines)

2. Hand out the questions about the topic.
3. Have students search for information in small teams. A friendly competition can even be set up to encourage participation.
4. Review answers as a class. Expand on the answers to enlarge the scope of learning.

VARIATIONS

1. Create questions that force students to *infer* answers from the resource information available rather than using questions that can be answered directly by the search.
2. Instead of hunting for answers to questions, give students a different task such as a case problem to solve, an exercise in which they have to match items, or a set of scrambled words that, if unscrambled, denote important terms contained in the resource information.

45
The Study Group

OVERVIEW

This method gives students the responsibility to study learning material and to clarify its contents as a group without the teacher's presence. The assignment needs to be specific enough to ensure that the resulting study session will be effective and the group will be self-managing.

PROCEDURE

1. Give students a short, well-formatted instructional handout; a brief text; or an interesting chart or diagram. Ask them to read it silently. A study group works best when the material is moderately challenging or open to widespread interpretation.
2. Form subgroups and give them a quiet space to conduct their study session.
3. Provide clear instructions that guide students to study and explicate the material carefully. Include directions such as these:

   - **Clarify** the contents.
   - **Create** examples, illustrations, or applications of the information or ideas.
   - **Identify** points that are confusing or with which you disagree.
   - **Argue** with the text; develop an opposing point of view.
   - **Assess** how well you understand the material.

   Here is an example:

   ### The Steps of Cardiopulmonary Resuscitation (CPR)
   a. Survey the scene.
   b. Check for unresponsiveness.
   c. Call for help.
   d. Open the airway.
   e. Look, listen, and feel for breathing.
   f. Give two breaths.
   g. Check for pulse.
   h. Give 15 chest compressions (if an adult), then two breaths.
   i. Repeat three times.
   j. Recheck the pulse. If none, return to step d.

   Discuss each step.
   Come up with an illustration of each step.
   Which steps do you want me to clarify or demonstrate?

Here is a different example:

> ### *The Fundamentals of Impressionism*
> A. **Impersonality:** The artist is honestly indifferent to the subject matter and creates pictures in which the artist's feelings are utterly uninvolved.
>   Discuss.
>   Give an example.
>   How well do you understand this concept?   1 2 3 4 5
> B. **Light:** Artists sought to create the illusion of forms bathed in light and atmosphere, requiring an intensive study of light as the source of color.
>   Discuss.
>   Give an example.
>   How well do you understand this concept?   1 2 3 4 5
> C. **Perception:** The artist records his own sensations of color, rather than painting the world as we presumably see it.
>   Discuss.
>   Give an example.
>   How well do you understand this concept?   1 2 3 4 5

4. Assign jobs to group members such as facilitator, timekeeper, recorder, or spokesperson (see "Ten Alternatives in Selecting Group Leaders and Filling Other Jobs," page 23).

5. Reconvene the total class and do one or more of the following:

   - Review the material together.
   - Quiz students.
   - Obtain questions.
   - Ask students to assess how well they understand the material.
   - Provide an application exercise or a quiz for students to test their understanding.

VARIATIONS

1. Do not form subgroups. Read aloud the material as a total class in the spirit of a "Bible study group." Stop the reading to answer student questions, pose questions of your own, or expound on the text.

2. If the class is large enough, create four or six study groups. Pair up study groups and ask them to compare notes and help each other.

46
Card Sort

OVERVIEW

This is a collaborative activity that can be used to teach concepts, classification characteristics, facts about objects, or review information. The physical movement featured can help to energize a tired class.

PROCEDURE

1. Give each students an index card containing information or an example that fits into one or more categories. Here are some examples:

   - Types of deciduous trees vs. types of evergreens
   - Characters in various Shakespearean plays
   - Powers of the executive, legislative, and judicial branches of government
   - Symptoms of different illnesses
   - Information that fits into varied parts of a job résumé
   - The characteristics of different metals
   - Nouns, verbs, adverbs, prepositions
   - Books by Dickens, Faulkner, Hemingway, and Updike

2. Ask students to mill around the room and find others whose card fits the same category. (You may announce the categories beforehand or let students discover them.)
3. Have students with cards in the same category present themselves to the rest of the class.
4. As each category is presented, make any teaching points you think are important.

VARIATIONS

1. Ask each group to make a teaching presentation about its category.
2. At the beginning of the activity, form teams. Give each team a complete set of cards. Be sure they are shuffled so that the categories into which they are to be sorted are not obvious. Ask each team to sort the cards into categories. Each team can obtain a score for the number of cards sorted correctly.

47

Learning Tournament

OVERVIEW

This technique is a simplified version of "Teams–Games–Tournaments," developed by Robert Slavin and his associates. It combines a study group and team competition and can be used to promote the learning of a wide variety of facts, concepts, and skills.

PROCEDURE

1. Divide students into teams with 2 to 8 members. Make sure the teams have equal numbers. (If this cannot be achieved, you will have to average each team's score.)
2. Provide teams with material to study together.
3. Develop several questions that test comprehension and/or recall of the learning material. Use formats that make self-scoring easy, such as multiple choice, fill in the blanks, true/false, or terms to define. In a computer class, for example, students are given terms such as the following to learn:

Cascade:	A way of arranging open windows
Icon:	Graphical representation of elements
Multitasking:	A computer's ability to run more than one thing at a time
Path:	Location of a file within the directory tree
Server:	A computer that provides disk space or printers to other computers
Attributes:	Information about a file

4. Give a portion of the questions to students. Refer to this as "round one" of the learning tournament. **Each student must answer the questions individually.**
5. After the questions have been given, provide the answers and ask students to count the number they answered correctly. Then have them pool their scores with every other member of their team to obtain a team score. Announce the scores of each team.
6. Ask the team to study again for the second round of the tournament. Then ask more test questions as part of "round two." Have teams once again pool their scores and add them to their round one score.
7. You can have as many rounds as you would like, but **be sure to allow the team to have a study session between each round.** (The length of a learning tournament can also vary. It might be as short as twenty minutes or as long as several hours.)

VARIATIONS

1. Penalize students for wrong answers by assigning them a score of -2 or -3. If they are unsure of the answer, a blank answer can be counted as 0.
2. Make the performance of a series of skills the basis of the tournament.

48

The Power of Two

OVERVIEW

This activity is used to promote cooperative learning and reinforce the importance and benefits of synergy—that is, that two heads are indeed better than one.

PROCEDURE

1. Give students one or more questions that require reflection and thinking. Here are some examples:

    - How do our bodies digest food?
    - What is knowledge?
    - What is "due process"?
    - How is the human brain like a computer?
    - Why do bad things sometimes happen to good people?

2. Ask students to answer the questions individually.
3. After all students have completed their answers, arrange into pairs and ask them to share their answers with each other.
4. Ask the pairs to create a new answer to each question, improving on each individual's response.
5. When all pairs have written new answers, compare the answers of each pair to the others in the class.

VARIATIONS
1. Invite the entire class to select the best answer for each question.
2. To save time, assign specific questions to specific pairs rather than having all pairs answer all questions.

49
Team Quiz

OVERVIEW

This team technique increases the students' accountability for what they are learning in a fun and nonthreatening way.

PROCEDURE

1. Choose a topic that can be presented in three segments.
2. Divide the students into three teams.
3. Explain the format of the session and start the presentation. Limit it to 10 minutes or less.
4. Have Team A prepare a short-answer quiz. The quiz should take no more than 5 minutes to prepare. Teams B and C use this time to review their notes.
5. Team A quizzes a member of Team B. If Team B cannot answer a question, Team C gets a shot at it.
6. Team A directs its next question to a member of Team C, and repeats the process.
7. When the quiz is over, continue with the second segment of your lesson, and appoint Team B as quizmasters.
8. After Team B completes its quiz, continue with the third segment of your lesson, and appoint Team C as quizmaster.

VARIATIONS

1. Give teams prepared quiz questions from which they select when it is their turn to be quizmaster.
2. Conduct one continuous lesson. Divide students into two teams. At the end of the lesson, have the two teams quiz each other.

Peer Teaching

Some experts believe that a subject is truly mastered only when a learner is able to teach it to someone else. Peer teaching gives students the opportunity to learn something well and, at the same time, become a resource to each other. The strategies that follow are practical ways to create peer teaching in the classroom. They also allow the teacher to supplement when necessary the teaching done by students.

50
Group-to-Group Exchange

OVERVIEW

In this strategy, different assignments are given to different groups of students. Each group then "teaches" what it has learned to the rest of the class.

PROCEDURE

1. Select a topic that includes different ideas, events, positions, concepts, or approaches to assign. The topic should be one that promotes an exchange of views or information (as opposed to a debate). Here are some examples:

   - Two famous battles during the Civil War
   - The ideas of two or more writers
   - Stages of child development
   - Different ways to improve nutrition
   - Different operating systems for computers

2. Divide the class into groups corresponding to the number of assignments. In most cases, two to four groups are appropriate for this activity. Give each sufficient time to prepare how they could present the topic they have been assigned. For example, one group might present a book by James Baldwin, and a second group might present a book by Toni Morrison.

3. When the preparation phase is completed, ask groups to select a spokesperson. Invite each spokesperson to address the other group(s).

4. After a brief presentation, encourage students to ask questions of the presenter or to offer their own views. Allow other members of the spokesperson's group to respond.

5. Continue the remaining presentations so that each group has given its information and has responded to audience questions and comments. Compare and contrast the views and information that were exchanged. For example, a teacher conducts a comparison of two countries that have been assigned, using this method. One group has been assigned Costa Rica (known as a peaceful country) and the other has been assigned El Salvador (recently ravaged by civil war). After each group presents the assigned country's culture and history, a discussion is held to analyze why two neighboring countries have had such a different experience.

VARIATIONS

1. Ask groups to do extensive research before their presentations.
2. Use a panel or fishbowl discussion format for each of the subgroups' presentations.

51
Jigsaw Learning

OVERVIEW

Jigsaw learning is a widely practiced technique that is similar to group-to-group exchange with one important difference: Every single student teaches something. It is an exciting alternative whenever there is material to be learned that can be segmented or "chunked" and when no one segment must be taught before the others. Each student learns something which, when combined with the material learned by others, forms a coherent body of knowledge or skill.

PROCEDURE

1. Choose learning material that can be broken into parts. A segment can be as short as one sentence or as long as several pages. (If the material is lengthy, ask students to read their assignment before class.)
    Examples include:

    - A multipoint handout
    - Parts of a science experiment
    - A text that has different sections or subheadings
    - A list of definitions
    - A group of magazine-length articles or other kinds of short reading material

2. Count the number of learning segments and the number of students. In an equitable manner, give out different assignments to different groups of students. For example, imagine a class of 12 students. Assume that you can divide learning materials into three segments or chunks. You might then be able to form quartets, assigning each group either segment 1, 2, or 3. Then, ask each quartet or "study group" to read, discuss, and learn the material assigned to them. (If you wish, you can form two pairs of "study buddies" first and then combine the pairs into the quartet to consult and share with each other.)

3. After the study period, form "jigsaw learning" groups. Such groups contain a representative of every "study group" in the class.* In the example just given, the members of each quartet could count off 1, 2, 3, and 4. Then form jigsaw learning groups of students with the same number. The result will be four trios. In each trio will be one person who has studied segment 1, one for segment 2, and one for segment 3. The following diagram displays this sequence.

Total Group Explanation

Study Group

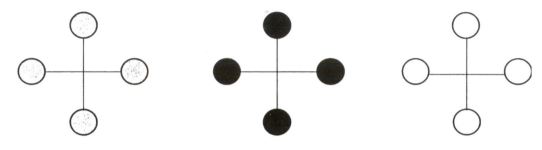

Cooperative Learning Groups

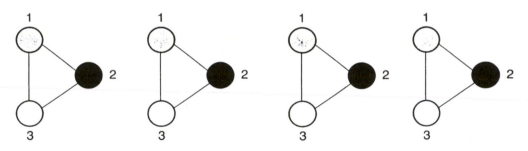

4. Ask the members of the "jigsaw" groups to teach each other what they have learned.
5. Reconvene the full class for review and remaining questions to ensure accurate understanding.

VARIATIONS

1. Assign a new task, such as answering a group of questions, that depends on the accumulated knowledge of all the members of a jigsaw learning group.
2. Assign to different students the responsibility to learn a skill rather than cognitive information. Have students teach one another the skills they have learned.

---

*In many instances, the number of students cannot be divided evenly into the number of learning segments. If this is the case, you can adjust by using learning partners instead of subgroups. Divide the learning material into only two segments, assigning one segment to one member of a pair and the other segment to his or her partner. For example, in a seven-part assignment, one person can be assigned parts 1–4 and the partner can be assigned parts 5–7. You can easily create study buddies with the same assignment. Then have the original pair teach each other what they have studied.

52

Everyone Is a Teacher Here

OVERVIEW

This is an easy strategy for obtaining classwide participation and individual accountability. It gives every student the opportunity to act as a "teacher" for other students.

PROCEDURE

1. Hand out an index card to each student. Ask students to write down a question they have about the learning material being studied in the class (e.g., a reading assignment) or a specific topic they would like discussed in class.

   In a class on American short stories, for example, the teacher might set the foundation for class discussion on Shirley Jackson's story "The Lottery" by distributing index cards and asking students to write down a question they have about the story. Here are some of the questions submitted by students and then redistributed to the class for response:

   a. *Whom were the villagers attempting to please by holding the lottery?*
   b. *How did the ritual of the lottery start?*
   c. *Why didn't anyone stop the stoning?*
   d. *Why was Mr. Summers in charge of the lottery?*

2. Collect the cards, shuffle them, and distribute one to each student. Ask students to read silently the question or topic on their card and think of a response.
3. Invite volunteers who are willing to read out loud the card they obtained and give a response.
4. After a response is given, ask the others in the class to add to what the volunteer has contributed.
5. Continue as long as there are volunteers.

VARIATIONS

1. Hold onto the cards you collect. Create a panel of respondents. Read each card and ask for discussion. Rotate the members of the panel frequently.
2. Ask students to write down on cards an opinion or observation they have about the learning material. Have other students agree or disagree with the opinion or observation.

53
Peer Lessons

OVERVIEW

This is a strategy to promote peer teaching in the classroom that places the entire responsibility for teaching fellow students on class members.

PROCEDURE

1. Divide the class into subgroups. Create as many subgroups as you have topics to be taught.
2. Give each group some information, a concept, or a skill to teach others. Here are some examples of topics:

   - The structure of an effective paragraph
   - Psychological defense mechanisms
   - Solving a math puzzle
   - The spread of AIDS

   The topics you provide to your students should be interrelated.
3. Ask each group to design a way to present or teach its topic to the rest of the class. Advise them to avoid lecturing or reading a report. Urge them to make the learning experience for students as active as possible.
4. Make some of the following suggestions:

   - Provide visual aids.
   - Develop a demonstration skit (where appropriate).
   - Use examples and/or analogies to make teaching points.
   - Involve students through discussion, quiz games, writing tasks, role playing, mental imagery, or case study.
   - Allow for questions.

For example, a teacher assigns a sociology class to develop classroom presentations on four major issues of *aging*. Four subgroups are formed and choose the following formats for peer teaching:

   - *The Aging Process:* A true/false quiz game on facts of aging
   - *Physical Aspects of Aging:* A simulation of typical aspects of aging (e.g., arthritis, decreased hearing, blurred vision)
   - *Stereotypes of Aging:* A writing task in which class members write about society's perceptions of the elderly

- *Loss of Independence:* A role play exercise involving an adult child discussing issues of transition with his or her parent

You might also select some methods from *Active Learning* as teaching strategies.

5. Allow sufficient time for planning and preparation (either in class or outside class). Then, have each group present their lessons. Applaud their efforts.

VARIATIONS

1. Instead of group teaching, have students teach or tutor others individually or in small groups.
2. Allow groups to give the class a prereading assignment before their lessons.

54
Student-Created Case Studies

OVERVIEW

Case study is widely heralded as one of the best learning methods. A typical case discussion focuses on the issues involved in a concrete situation or example, the action that should be taken and the lessons that can be learned, and the ways of handling or avoiding such situations in the future. The technique that follows allows students to create their own case studies.

PROCEDURE

1. Divide the class into pairs or trio. Invite them to develop a case study that the remainder of the class could analyze and discuss.

2. Indicate that the purpose of a case study is to learn about a topic by examining a concrete situation or example that reflects that topic. Following are some examples:

   - A haiku poem can be written to show how it's done.
   - An actual résumé can be analyzed to study how to write a résumé.
   - An account of how someone conducted a scientific experiment can be discussed to learn about scientific procedures.
   - A dialogue between a manager and an employee can be examined to learn how to provide positive reinforcement.
   - The steps taken by a parent in a conflict situation with a child can be studied to learn about behavior management.

3. Provide adequate time for the pairs or trios to develop a short case situation or example that poses an example or issue to be discussed or a problem to be solved that is relevant to the subject matter of the class.

   In a class on twentieth-century U.S. history, for example, the teacher might select three different historical events in which the United States intervened overseas and assign one to each pair of students so that each may develop a case study to review American foreign policy.

   These are:
   1. Bay of Pigs invasion
   2. Intervention of troops in Vietnam
   3. Assignment of troops to Somalia

Each pair then writes a summary case study specifically detailing the events that led to the decision to send U.S. troops overseas. Questions for analysis are:

- *What were the primary reasons for U.S. intervention?*
- *How well informed was the U.S. public about the decision?*
- *Who made the decision?*
- *What precedents were set for U.S. foreign policy?*

4. When the case studies are complete, have the groups present them to the class. Allow a member of the group to lead the case discussion.

VARIATIONS

1. Obtain a small number of volunteers who prepare case studies in advance for the rest of the class. (The preparation of a case study is an excellent learning assignment.)
2. Create an even number of groups. Pair up groups and have them exchange case studies.

55
In the News

OVERVIEW

This is an interesting way to get students involved and arouse their interest in the topic even before they attend the class. This peer teaching approach will also result in a wealth of material and information that can be shared with all students.

PROCEDURE

1. Ask students to bring to class articles, news items, editorials, and cartoons related to the topic of the class session. For example, a teacher can request that students bring in a newspaper or magazine story about weather, such as a discussion of global warming.
2. Divide the class into subgroups and ask them to share their items with each other and choose the two or three most interesting.
3. Reconvene the entire class and ask representatives from each subgroup to share their choices with other students.
4. As groups are reporting, listen for important points that you will address in the class and use that information to promote discussion.

VARIATIONS

1. Collect all items from the students, copy them, and distribute them as a follow-up to the class session. Or ask students to submit their items prior to the class. You could then copy them and send them to all students as prereading assignments.
2. Use the news items as case studies or the basis of role plays.

56
Poster Session

OVERVIEW

This alternative presentation method is an excellent way to inform students quickly, capture their imaginations, and invite an exchange of ideas among them. This technique is also a novel and graphic way of enabling students to express their perceptions and feelings about the topic you are currently discussing in a nonthreatening environment.

PROCEDURE

1. Ask every student to select a topic related to the general class topic or unit being discussed or studied.
2. Request that students prepare a visual display of their concept on a poster board or bulletin board. (You will determine the size.) The poster display should be self-explanatory; that is, observers would easily understand the idea without any further written or oral explanation. However, students may choose to prepare a one-page handout to accompany the poster offering more detail and to serve as further reference material.
3. During the designated class session, ask students to post their visual presentations and freely circulate around the room viewing and discussing each other's posters.

A health class, for example, is studying stress. Topics that are assigned include the following:

- *Causes of stress*
- *Symptoms of stress*
- *Effects of stress on self and others*
- *Stress reducers*

One of the students illustrates the symptoms of stress by creating a poster display that shows the following pictures:

- *An overweight person on a scale*
- *Someone drinking an alcoholic drink*
- *Two people arguing*
- *A person with a headache*

Below each picture is a short paragraph explaining how and why a stressed person might be exhibiting the symptom portrayed.

4. Fifteen minutes before the end of the class, convene the entire class and discuss what they found valuable about the activity.

VARIATIONS

1. You may choose to form teams of two or three instead of making individual assignments, particularly if the topic is limited in scope.
2. Follow up a poster session with a panel discussion, using some displayers as panelists.

Independent Learning

Full-class and collaborative learning can be enhanced by independent learning activity. When students learn on their own, they develop the ability to focus and reflect. Working on their own also gives them the opportunity to take personal responsibility for their learning. The strategies that follow are a combination of techniques that can be used inside and outside the classroom.

57

Imagine

OVERVIEW

Through visual imagery, students can create their own ideas. Imagery is effective as a creative supplement to collaborative learning. It can also serve as a springboard to an independent project that may initially seem overwhelming to students.

PROCEDURES

1. Introduce the topic that will be covered. Explain to students that the subject requires creativity and that the use of visual imagery may assist their efforts.
2. Instruct the class to close their eyes. Introduce a relaxation exercise that will clear current thoughts from the students' minds. Use background music, dimmed lights, and breathing to achieve results.
3. Conduct warm-up exercises to open the mind's eye. Ask students, with their eyes closed, to try to visualize sights and sounds such as a rosebud, their bedroom, a changing traffic light, or the patter of rain.
4. When class members are relaxed and warmed up, provide an image for them to build upon. Suggestions include:

   - A future experience
   - An unfamiliar setting
   - A problem to solve
   - A project that lies ahead

   For example, a teacher is helping students prepare for a job interview. Students are asked the following questions:

   - *What are you wearing?*
   - *What time of day is it?*
   - *What does the office look like?*
   - *What kind of chair are you sitting on?*
   - *Where is the interviewer sitting?*
   - *What does the interviewer look like?*
   - *How do you feel?*
   - *What does the interviewer ask you? How do you respond?*

5. As the image is described, provide regular silent intervals so that students can build their own visual image. Build in questions that encourage the use of all senses, such as:

- What does it look like?
- Whom do you see? What are they doing?
- What do you feel?

6. Conclude guiding the image and instruct class members to remember their image. Slowly end the exercise.
7. Ask students to form small groups and to share their imagery experiences. Ask them to describe to one another the image using as many senses as possible. Or ask them to write about it.

VARIATIONS

1. Now that students have rehearsed in their minds how they would act in a specific situation, invite them to plan out how they might actually act on their thoughts.
2. Conduct an imagery exercise in which students experience failure. Then have them imagine a success.

58
Writing in the Here and Now

OVERVIEW

Writing allows students to reflect on experiences they have had. A dramatic way to promote independent reflection is to ask students to write a present-tense action account of an experience they have had (as if it were happening in the here and now).

PROCEDURE

1. Select the kind of experience you want students to write about. It can be a past or future event. Among the possibilities might be:

   - A recent problem
   - A family event
   - A first day on a new job
   - A presentation
   - An experience with a friend
   - A learning situation

2. Inform students about the experience you have selected for the purpose of reflective writing. Tell them that a valuable way to reflect on the experience is to relive it or experience it for the first time in the here and now. Doing so makes the impact clearer and more dramatic than writing about something in the "there and then" or in the distant future.

3. Provide a clear, firm surface on which to write. Establish privacy and quiet.

4. Ask students to write, in the present tense, about the experience selected. Have them begin at the start of the experience and write what they and others are doing and feeling, such as, "I am standing before classmates giving a presentation. I really want to appear confident . . ." Invite students to write as much as they wish about the events that occur and the feelings that are generated.

5. Allow enough time for writing. Students should not feel rushed. When they are finished, invite them to read over their reflections in the here and now.

6. Discuss what new actions they might undertake in the future.

VARIATIONS

1. To help students get in the mood for reflective writing, first conduct a mental imagery exercise or hold a group discussion relevant to the topic you are assigning.
2. Ask students to share what they have written. One alternative is to invite a limited number of volunteers to read their finished work. A second alternative is to have partners share their writing with each other.

59
Mind Maps

OVERVIEW

Mind mapping is a creative way for individual students to generate ideas, record learning, or plan a new project. Asking students to create a mind map enables them to identify clearly and creatively what they have learned or what they are planning.

PROCEDURE

1. Select the topic for mind mapping. Some possibilities include:

    *   A problem or issue about which you want students to create action ideas
    *   A concept or skill you have just taught
    *   A project to be planned by the students

2. Construct for the class a simple mind map using color, images, or symbols. One example would be a trip to the grocery store during which a person shops from a mind map that categorizes items needed according to the departments in which they are found (e.g., dairy, produce, and frozen foods). Explain how the colors, images, and symbols in your mind map promote whole brain thinking (versus right brain/left brain thinking). Invite students to cite simple examples from their daily lives that they could mind map.

3. Provide paper, marking pens, and any other resources you think will help students to create colorful, graphic mind maps. Give students the mind-mapping assignment. Suggest that they begin their maps by creating a pictorial center, depicting the topic or main idea. Then, encourage them to break the whole into smaller components and depict these components around the periphery of the map (using color and graphics). **Urge them to represent each idea pictorially, using as few words as possible.** Following this, they can elaborate as details pop into their minds.

4. Provide plenty of time for students to develop their mind maps. Encourage them to look at other people's work to stimulate ideas.

5. Ask students to share their mind maps. Conduct a discussion about the value of this creative way to outline ideas.

VARIATIONS

1. Assign a team mind map instead of students working individually.
2. Use computers to generate mind maps.

60
Action Learning

OVERVIEW

Action learning gives students an opportunity to experience firsthand in a real-life setting the application of the topic and content being studied or discussed in class. An outside-class project puts them in the discovery mode and enables them to be creative in sharing their discoveries with the class. The beauty of this activity is that it can be used with any subject or application.

PROCEDURE

1. Introduce the topic to the students by providing some background information through a brief lecture-based lesson and class discussion.
2. Explain that you are going to give them an opportunity to experience the topic firsthand by making a "field trip" to a real-life setting.
3. Divide the class into subgroups of four or five and ask them to develop a list of questions and/or specific things they should look for during their "field trip."
4. Ask the subgroups to post their questions or checklist items and share them with the rest of the class.
5. The class will then discuss the items and develop a common list for every person to use.
6. Give students a deadline (e.g., one week) and direct them to visit a site or sites and to use their list of questions or checklist items to interview or observe. They may choose their own sites, or you may want to make specific assignments to avoid duplication or to get good distribution. For example, students might be asked to visit businesses such as a retail store, a fast food restaurant, a hotel, or an auto repair shop. They would then visit these businesses as customers to see how they are treated.
7. Questions should be specific and lend themselves to comparison with each other's findings.

   For example, with customer service, the following observation items would be appropriate:
   - *How long did the employee take before acknowledging the customer?*
   - *Did the employee smile?*
   - *Was the employee courteous and polite?*
   - *Did the employee ask open-ended questions to identify the problem?*

- *Did the employee use active listening techniques? Give examples.*
- *Did the employee resolve the problem?*
- *Were you, as the customer, pleased with the experience? Why or why not?*

8. Ask the students to share their findings with the rest of the class through some clever or creative method (e.g., a skit, a mock interview, a panel discussion, or a game).

VARIATIONS

1. You may want to form teams of two or three students instead of giving individual assignments.
2. Instead of the class developing a common list of questions or observation guidelines, individuals could develop their own lists.

61

Learning Journals

OVERVIEW

When students are asked to reflect in writing about the learning experiences they have undergone, they are encouraged to become conscious, through language, of what is happening to them. A widely used technique in this regard is a learning journal, a reflective log or diary students keep over time.

PROCEDURE

1. Explain to students that experience is not necessarily the best teacher and that it is important to reflect on experiences to become conscious of what those experiences have taught them.
2. Invite students (or require them, if appropriate) to keep a journal of their reflections and learnings.
3. Suggest that they write, twice a week, some of their thoughts and feelings about what they are learning. Tell them to record these comments as a personal diary (without worrying about spelling, grammar, and punctuation).
4. Ask students to focus on some or all of the following categories:

   - What's been **unclear** to them or what they **disagree** with
   - How the learning experiences **connect** with their personal lives
   - How the learning experiences are **reflected** in other things they read, see, or do
   - What they have **observed** about themselves or others since the learning experiences
   - What they **concluded** from the learning experiences
   - What they would like to **do** as a result of the learning experiences

5. Collect, read, and comment on the journals periodically so that students are held accountable for keeping them and so that you can receive feedback about their learnings.

VARIATIONS

1. Instead of a blank notebook, a structured form can be provided on which students can organize their journal entries.
2. Ask students to write during class time rather than after class.

62
Learning Contracts

OVERVIEW

Learning that is self-directed is often deeper and more permanent than teacher-directed learning. However, you should make sure that the agreements about what and how something will be learned are made explicit. One means to accomplish this is the learning contract.

PROCEDURE

1. Ask each student to select a topic he or she wants to study independently.
2. Encourage each student to think carefully through the plan of study. Allow plenty of time for research and consultation in drawing up the plan.
3. Request of the student a written contract that covers the following categories:

   - The learning objectives the student wants to attain
   - The specific knowledge or skills to be mastered
   - The learning activities that will be utilized
   - The evidence the student will present to show that the objectives have been achieved
   - A completion date

Following is a contract created by a student who wants to work on his résumé.

Topic:	Résumé Writing
Learning objectives:	• Present myself in a favorable light on paper.
Specific knowledge:	• Choose an appropriate format. • Condense four pages into two. • Write a clear career objective.
Learning activities:	• Review sample résumés. • Choose those that I like and comment on them. • Prepare a draft from critique by teacher. • Rewrite as necessary. • Send copies to three people and ask them to comment. • Prepare final résumé.
Completion date:	• Within two weeks

4. Meet with the student and discuss the proposed contract. Suggest learning resources available to the student. Negotiate any changes you would like to make.

VARIATIONS

1. Create group learning contracts instead of individual ones.
2. Instead of giving freedom of choice, select the topic and objectives for the student or offer a limited selection. However, allow greater choice about how the topic will be studied.

Affective Learning

Affective learning activities help students to examine their feelings, values, and attitudes. Even the most technical topics involve affective learning. For example, what good are computer skills if students are anxious and unsure of themselves when they use a computer? The strategies that follow are designed to bring into awareness the feelings, values, and attitudes that accompany many classroom topics. They gently push students into examining their beliefs and asking themselves if they are committed to new ways of doing things.

63

Seeing How It Is

OVERVIEW

Often, a topic promotes understanding of and sensitivity to people or situations that are unfamiliar to students. One of the best ways to accomplish this goal is to create an affective activity that simulates what that unfamiliar person or situation is like.

PROCEDURE

1. Choose a type of person or situation that you want students to learn about. Here are some examples:

   - What it's like to be in the minority
   - What it's like to be in a different time period in history
   - What it's like to be from a different culture
   - What it's like to be a person with special problems or challenges

2. Create a way to simulate that person or situation. Among the ways to do this are the following:

   - Have students dress in the attire of that person or situation. Or have them handle the equipment, props, accessories, or other belongings of that person or situation or engage in a typical activity of that person.

     For example, sensitize students to the normal process of aging by giving them eyeglasses smeared with Vaseline, dried peas to put in each shoe, cotton for each ear, and latex gloves for both hands. Then ask them to take out a pencil and paper and write down their name, address, and telephone number, or to take a walk outside the classroom, open the door, and find their way around.

   - Place students in situations in which they are required to respond as the role or character they have been given.
   - Use an analogy to build a simulation: Create a scenario with which students may be familiar that sheds light on the unfamiliar situation. For example, you might ask all students who are left-handed to portray people who are culturally different from the rest of the students.
   - Impersonate an individual and ask the students to interview you and find out about your experiences, views, and feelings.

For example, a science teacher (Kate Brooks) dresses as Galileo and presents a play about his life and the ethical dilemmas he faced. Renaissance music is played and candles burn in the planetarium, while Galileo makes discoveries with the telescope. The play ends with Galileo's trial and defense of his teachings. At the play's conclusion, students write an essay about the ethical questions Galileo faces, give their view of his decisions, and guess at what they would have done.

3. Ask students how the simulation felt. Discuss the experience of being in someone else's shoes. Invite students to identify the challenges that unfamiliar persons and situations present to them.

VARIATIONS

1. If possible, arrange for real encounters with the unfamiliar situation or person.
2. Conduct a mental imagery experience in which students visualize the person or situation with which they are unfamiliar.

64
Billboard Ranking

OVERVIEW

Many learning situations contain no right or wrong content. When values, opinions, ideas, and preferences exist about a topic you are teaching, this activity can be used to stimulate reflection and discussion.

PROCEDURE

1. Divide the class into subgroups of four to six students.
2. Give students a list of any of the following:

   - Values they may hold (e.g., 1. *loyalty*, 2. . . . , etc.)
   - Opinions they may espouse (e.g., 1. *Crime prevention should be our major national concern*, 2. . . . , etc.)
   - Alternative solutions to a problem (e.g., *Save energy by:* 1. *carpooling*, 2. . . . , etc.)
   - Decision choices they or others face (e.g., 1. *Legalize drugs*, 2. . . . , etc.)
   - Attributes they desire (e.g., 1. *good-looking*, 2. . . . , etc.)
   - Preferences they hold (e.g., 1. *Edgar Allan Poe*, 2. . . . , etc.)

   For example, students might be asked what qualities they want in a friend: *reliable, funny, cool, understanding*, etc.
3. Give each subgroup a Post-it™ pad. Ask them to write each item on the list on a separate sheet.
4. Next ask the subgroups to sort the sheets so that the value, opinion, or action they most prefer is on top and the remaining are placed consecutively in rank order.
5. Create a "billboard" on which subgroups can display their rank order preferences. (The Post-it notes can be attached to a blackboard, a flip chart, or a large piece of paper.)
6. Compare and contrast the rankings across groups that are now visually displayed.

VARIATIONS

1. Attempt to achieve a classwide consensus.
2. Ask students to interview members of groups whose rankings differ from theirs.

65

What? So What? Now What?

OVERVIEW

The value of any experiential learning activity is enhanced by asking students to reflect on the experience they just had and explore its implications. This reflection period is often referred to as processing *or* debriefing. *Some experiential teachers now use the term* harvesting. *Here is a three-stage sequence for harvesting a rich learning experience.*

PROCEDURE

1. Take the class through an experience that is appropriate to your topic. These experiences might include any of the following:

   - A game or simulation exercise
   - A field trip
   - A video
   - An action learning project
   - A debate
   - A role play
   - A mental imagery exercise

2. Ask students to share **what** happened to them during the experience:

   - What did they do?
   - What did they observe? Think about?
   - What feelings did they have during the experience?

   Use any of the options listed in "Ten Methods to Get Participation at Any Time," page 16, to generate responses.

3. Next ask students to ask themselves, **"So what?"**

   - What benefits did they get from the experience?
   - What did they learn? Relearn?
   - What are the implications of the activity?
   - How does the experience (if it is a simulation or role play) relate to the real world?

4. Finally, ask students to consider **"Now what?"**

   - How do you want to do things differently in the future?
   - How can you extend the learning you had?
   - What steps can you take to apply what you have learned?

VARIATIONS

1. Limit the discussion to "What?" and "So what?"
2. Use these questions to stimulate journal writing (see strategy 61, "Learning Journals").

66

Active Self-Assessment

OVERVIEW

Through this method, the students are able to share their attitudes about a subject through self-assessment. It allows the teacher to gauge feelings and beliefs of the students and serves as a springboard for class discussion.

PROCEDURE

1. Create a list of statements that will be read to the class to assess their attitudes and feelings about a given subject.

    For example, a teacher composes the following statements:
    *   *I want a job that allows me to work with other people.*
    *   *I want a job that pays me the most I can get, given my skills.*
    *   *I want a job that is secure and free from worry about being constantly evaluated.*
    *   *I want a job that I don't have to take home at night.*
    *   *I want a job that doesn't involve a lot of commuting and travel.*
    *   *I want a job that has value to the community.*
    *   *I want a job that constantly challenges my abilities.*

2. Ask the students to stand in the back of the room, clearing away the chairs or desks to one side.
3. Create a rating scale of numbers one through five in the front of the room by using the blackboard or posting numbers on the wall.
4. Explain that statements will be read to the class. After hearing each one, the students should stand in front of the rating number that best matches their attitude about or knowledge of the subject. Depending on the subject matter, number 1 could be "Strongly Agree" or "Fully Understand," with the range extending to 5 for "Strongly Disagree" or "Do Not Understand."
5. As each statement is read, students should move to the place in the room that best matches their knowledge or opinion. After lines form in front of the various positions, invite some students to share why they have chosen that position.
6. After hearing the opinions of others, invite any students who wish to alter their position on the scale to do so.
7. Continue reading the individual statements or facts and requesting that students move to the number that best matches their opinion or knowledge.

8. Next, break students into subgroups. Give them a written copy of the statements and ask them to discuss them.
9. Now, ask students to reconsider privately their stand on each item. Have them assign a number to each statement that reflects their final level of agreement or disagreement.

VARIATIONS

1. In a larger setting, have the students first choose a response to the statements and then move to the numbered posts.
2. Begin with small-group discussion and then proceed with individual (private) assessment.

67
Role Models

This activity is an interesting way to stimulate discussion about values and attitudes. Students are asked to nominate well-known personalities they see as role models of traits associated with a topic being studied in class.

PROCEDURE

1. Divide students into subgroups of five or six, and give each group a sheet of newsprint and markers.
2. Ask each group to identify three people they would identify as representative of the subject under discussion. In music, for example, they might choose Elton John, Billy Joel, and Stevie Wonder.
3. After they have identified the three well-known figures, ask them to make a list of the characteristics the three have in common that qualify them as examples or role models for the subject under discussion. They are to write their lists of people and characteristics on newsprint and post on the wall.
4. Reconvene the entire class and compare lists, asking each group to explain why they chose the people they did.
5. Lead the class in a discussion of the varied perceptions among the students.

VARIATIONS

1. Instead of citing real people, ask students to choose fictional characters.
2. Assign each subgroup a specific list of people who are representative of the subject under discussion.

Skill Development

One of the most important goals of education today is the acquisition of skills for the modern workplace. There are technical skills like writing and computing. There are also nontechnical skills, such as listening attentively and speaking clearly. When students are struggling to learn new skills and improve existing ones, they need to practice them effectively and to obtain useful feedback. The strategies that follow represent different ways to develop skills. Some are intense and some are fun. In particular, different role-playing designs are featured.

68
The Firing Line

OVERVIEW

This is a lively, fast-moving format that can be used for a variety of purposes, such as testing and role playing. It features continually rotating pairs. Students get the opportunity to respond to rapidly fired questions or other types of challenges.

PROCEDURE

1. Decide on the purpose for which you would like to use "the firing line." Here are some examples when your goal is skill development:

    *   Students can test or drill each other.
    *   Students can role-play a situation assigned to them.
    *   Students can teach each other.

    You can also use this strategy for other situations. Here are some examples:

    *   Students can interview others to obtain their views and opinions.
    *   Students can discuss a short text or quotation.

2. Arrange chairs in two facing rows. Have enough chairs for all the students in the class.

3. Separate the chairs into clusters of three to five on each side or row. The arrangement might look like this:

4. Distribute to each *x* student a card containing a task or assignment to which he or she will instruct the *y* person opposite him or her to respond. Use one of the following:

    *   An interview topic (e.g., ask the person opposite you this question: "How do you feel about the character of_____ in the book _____?")
    *   A test question (e.g., ask the person opposite you, "What is the formula for _____?")
    *   A short text or quotation (e.g., ask the person opposite you his or her opinion about the phrase "There is nothing so important you have to fight for it.")
    *   A character to role-play (e.g., ask the person opposite you to portray a person who must tell a friend not to drink and drive)
    *   A teaching assignment (e.g., ask the person opposite you to teach you when to use a colon and a semicolon)

    Give a different card to each *x* member of a cluster.

    For example, a teacher is training students to maintain good eye contact and speak fluently. The teacher gives to the x members of each cluster one of the following cards:
    *   *Ask the person opposite you to give his or her views about the current president of the United States.*
    *   *Ask the person opposite you to tell you about his or her childhood.*
    *   *Ask the person opposite you to explain the features and benefits of the toothpaste he or she uses.*
    *   *Ask the person opposite you to tell you about his or her hobbies and interests.*

5. Begin the first assignment. After a brief period of time, announce that it is time for all the *y*'s to rotate one chair to the left (or right) within the cluster. Do not rotate the *x*'s. Have the *x* person "fire" his or her assignment or task to the *y* person opposite him or her. Continue for as many rounds as you have different tasks.

VARIATIONS

1. Reverse roles so that the *x* students become the *y* students.
2. In some situations, it may be interesting and appropriate to give the same assignment to each cluster member. In this instance, the *y* student will be asked to respond to the same instructions for each member of his or her cluster. For example, a student could be asked to role-play the same situation a number of times.

69
Active Observation and Feedback

OVERVIEW

The usual procedure when utilizing observers in role-playing exercises or skill practice sessions is to wait until the performance is over before inviting feedback. This procedure gives performers immediate feedback. It also keeps observers on their toes during the performance.

PROCEDURE

1. Develop a role-playing exercise in which some students practice a skill while others observe them.
2. Provide the observers with a concrete checklist of positive and/or negative behaviors to notice. Instruct them to give a signal to the role players when the desired behaviors are occurring and a different signal when undesired behaviors take place. Signals that can be used are:

   * Raising hands
   * Whistling
   * Snapping fingers
   * Clapping

   Students in a class on conversational Spanish, for example, could use this activity to practice grammar. The teacher prepares ten different situations and has the role-playing participants choose one from a hat. Prior to the role-play beginning, the class chooses a signal for improper grammar (snap of the fingers) and one for positive reinforcement (wave of the hand). The two people role playing begin the dialogue in Spanish. If a grammatical error occurs, members of the audience may snap; to provide positive feedback, they wave. A variation to avoid constant interruption would be to call time at one-minute intervals and provide a general appraisal (number of snaps or waves) or instant rating.

3. Explain that the purpose of the signals is to provide **immediate feedback** to the role players concerning their performance.
4. Discuss the experience with the role players engaging in skill practice. Find out if the immediate feedback helped or hindered them.

VARIATIONS

1. Allow observers to use a signal (e.g., blowing a whistle) to freeze the action of the role play and ask questions or give more detailed feedback to the role players.
2. Videotape the role plays. Do not permit any active forms of observational feedback during the taping. Have students watch the tapes and use the established signals during the replay.

70

Nonthreatening Role Playing

OVERVIEW

This technique reduces the threat of role playing by placing the teacher in the lead role and involving the class in providing the responses and setting the scenario's direction.

PROCEDURE

1. Create a role play in which you will demonstrate desired behaviors, such as handling a person who is angry.
2. Inform the class that you will play the leading role in the role play. The students' job is to help you deal with the situation.
3. Obtain a student volunteer to role-play the other person in the situation (e.g., the angry person). Give that student an opening script to read to help him or her get into the role. Start the role play, but stop at frequent intervals and ask the class to give you feedback and direction as the scenario progresses. Don't hesitate to ask students to provide specific lines for you to use. For example, at a specific point, ask, "What should I say next?" Listen to suggestions from the audience and try one of them out.
4. Continue the role play so that students increasingly coach you how to handle the situation. This gives them skill practice while you do the actual role playing for them.

VARIATIONS

1. Using the same procedure, have the audience coach a fellow student (instead of the teacher).
2. Videotape the entire role play. Play it back and discuss with students other ways to respond at specific points in the situation.

71
Triple Role Playing

OVERVIEW

This technique expands traditional role playing by utilizing three different students in the same role-play situation. It shows the effect of individual style variation on the situation's outcome.

PROCEDURE

1. With the help of a willing student, demonstrate the basic technique of role playing (if needed) with a situation such as a student protesting a grade to a teacher.
2. Create the scenario and describe it to the class.
3. Ask for four students from the class to assume the character roles in the role play. Assign one person to remain as the standard character (e.g., the teacher) and instruct the remaining three individuals that they will all play the remaining role (e.g. the student) on a rotating basis.
4. Ask the three rotating volunteers to leave the room and decide the order in which they will participate. When ready, the first volunteer reenters the room and begins role playing with the standard volunteer.
5. After three minutes, call time and ask for the second volunteer to enter the room and repeat the same situation. The first volunteer may now remain in the room. After three minutes with the second volunteer, continue with the third volunteer repeating the scenario.
6. At the conclusion, ask the class to compare and contrast the styles of the three volunteers by identifying which techniques were effective and noting areas for improvement.

VARIATIONS

1. Instead of holding a classwide discussion, divide students into three groups. Assign one of the three role players to each group. Ask each group to give the person assigned to them supportive feedback. Use this procedure when you feel the need to reduce the potential embarrassment of comparing the role players publicly.
2. For a larger group, divide the class into three sections and follow the rotation of triple role playing, with the volunteers rotating among the three groups. The class can then reconvene to compare and contrast the three styles.

72
Rotating Roles

OVERVIEW

This activity is an excellent way of giving each student an opportunity to practice skills through role playing real-life situations.

PROCEDURE

1. Divide the class into groups of three spread throughout the room with as much space between groups as possible.
2. Ask each trio to create three real-life scenarios dealing with the topic you have been discussing.
3. After each trio has written its three scenarios on three separate sheets of paper, one team member from each group delivers the scenarios to the next group and is available as the group members read the scenarios to clarify or provide additional information if necessary. The student then returns to his or her original group.
4. On a rotating basis, each member of the trio will have an opportunity to practice the primary role (e.g., a parent), secondary role (e.g., a child), and observer.
5. Each round should consist of at least 10 minutes of role playing, with 5 to 10 minutes of feedback from the observer. You will determine the length of each round on the basis of your time constraints, the topic, and the students' skill level.
6. In each round, the observer should concentrate on identifying what the primary player did well in using the concepts and skills learned in the class and what he or she can do to improve.
7. After all three rounds have been completed, reconvene the entire group for general discussion of the key learning points and value of the activity.

VARIATIONS

1. You can prepare scenarios instead of having each group write them.
2. Prepare an observer feedback sheet identifying specific skills and techniques the observer should look for.

73
Modeling the Way

OVERVIEW

This technique gives students an opportunity to practice, through demonstration, specific skills taught in the class. Demonstration is often an appropriate alternative to role playing because it is less threatening. Students are given ample time to create their own scenarios and determine how they want to illustrate the skills and techniques just covered in the class.

PROCEDURE

1. Following learning activities on a given topic, identify several general situations where the students might be required to use the skills just discussed.
2. Divide the class into subgroups according to the number of participants necessary to demonstrate a given scenario. In most cases, two or three people will be required.
3. Give the subgroups 10 to 15 minutes to create a specific scenario illustrating general situations.
4. The subgroups will also determine how they are going to demonstrate the skill to the group. Give them 5 to 7 minutes to practice.
5. Each subgroup will take turns delivering its demonstration for the rest of the class. Allow the opportunity for feedback after each demonstration.

VARIATIONS

1. You can create subgroups of more people than are necessary for the demonstration, with those not performing serving as creators of the scenarios, directors, and advisers.
2. You can create the specific scenarios and assign them to specific subgroups.

74

Silent Demonstration

OVERVIEW

This is a strategy to use when you are teaching any kind of step-by-step procedure. By demonstrating a procedure as silently as possible, you encourage students to be mentally alert.

PROCEDURE

1. Decide on a multistep procedure you want students to learn. Procedures might include any of the following:

   - Using a computer application
   - Using lab equipment
   - Operating machinery
   - Giving first aid
   - Solving a mathematical problem
   - Searching reference material
   - Drawing and other artistic expressions
   - Repairing appliances
   - Applying an accounting procedure

2. Ask the students to watch you perform the entire procedure. Just do it, with little or no explanation or commentary about what and why you are doing what you do. Give them a visual glimpse of the big picture or the entire job. Do not expect retention. At this point, you are merely establishing readiness for learning.

3. Form pairs. Demonstrate the first part of the procedure, again with little or no explanation or commentary. **Ask pairs to discuss with each other what they observed you doing.** [Telling them what you are doing will lessen students' mental alertness.] Obtain a volunteer to explain what you did. If the students have difficulty, demonstrate again. Acknowledge correct observations.

4. Have the pairs practice with each other the first part of the procedure. When it is mastered, proceed with a silent demonstration of the next parts of the procedure, followed by paired practice.

5. End by challenging students to do the entire procedure without any help.

VARIATIONS

1. If possible, give students an opening task to attempt the procedure before any demonstration. Encourage guesses and an openness to making mistakes. By do-

ing this, you will immediately get students mentally involved. Then, have them watch you demonstrate.

2. If some students master the procedure sooner than others, recruit them as "silent demonstrators."

75

Practice-Rehearsal Pairs*

OVERVIEW

This is a simple strategy for practicing and rehearsing any skill or procedure with a learning partner. The goal is to ensure that both partners can perform the skill or procedure.

PROCEDURE

1. Select a set of skills or procedures you want students to master. Create pairs. Within each pair, assign two roles: (1) **explainer** or **demonstrator** and (2) **checker.**
2. The explainer or demonstrator explains and/or demonstrates how to perform any specified skill or procedure. The checker verifies that the explanation and/or demonstration is correct, encourages, and provides coaching if needed.
3. The partners reverse roles. The new explainer/demonstrator is given another skill or procedure to perform.
4. The process continues until all the skills are rehearsed.

VARIATIONS

1. Use a multistep skill or procedure instead of a set of several distinct ones. Have the explainer/demonstrator perform one step and have the partner perform the next step until the sequence of steps is completed.
2. When the pairs have completed their work, arrange a demonstration before any group.

---

*This technique is based on "Drill-Review Pairs" by David W. Johnson, Roger T. Johnson, and Karl A. Smith.

76

I Am the _____

OVERVIEW

In this strategy, students assume the role of a person whose job they are learning about. Students are given realistic on-the-job assignments with little prior instruction and learn "by doing."

PROCEDURE

1. Choose the role you want students to perform. Here are some examples:

   I am the   *mayor*
               visitor to (foreign country)
               editor
               historian
               scientist
               job applicant
               business owner
               researcher
               journalist

2. Prepare written instructions explaining one or several tasks that might be assigned to that role. For example, a mayor might be asked to bring a bill to the city council.
3. Pair up students and present the assignments to each pair. Give them a time allotment to finish the assignments. Provide reference material to support them as they attempt to deal with the assignments.
4. Reconvene the full class and discuss the assignments.

VARIATIONS

1. Allow students to leave the classroom and obtain coaching from fellow employees who can act as resources to them.
2. Have students do the tasks alone, without the support of a partner.

77

Curveballs

OVERVIEW

This is a dramatic way to practice job-related skills. It places students in difficult situations which they must figure how to escape or resolve.

PROCEDURE

1. Select a situation that is common to the job being studied by students. Examples might include:

   - Leading a meeting
   - Giving an assignment to an employee
   - Getting an assignment from a manager
   - Making a presentation
   - Giving a report to a manager
   - Talking to a customer

2. Recruit a volunteer who is willing to role-play a specific situation. Be sure to explain the situation in detail.

3. Hand out instructions to other students that direct them to throw "curveballs" at the volunteer. Specify some actions that can be taken to give the volunteer a difficult time handling the situation. Do not let the volunteer see the "curveball" instructions.

   In a job interview, for example, the applicant can be asked to reveal personal information (which is illegal). The applicant needs to decide how to respond.

4. Allow the volunteer to cope with the situation. Applaud his or her efforts. Discuss with the entire class ways to deal with the unanticipated events.

5. Recruit new volunteers and present different challenges to them.

VARIATIONS

1. Invite the students to select their own "curveballs" to throw at the volunteers.
2. Instead of using volunteers, demonstrate yourself how to handle the "curveballs" thrown by students.

78
Advisory Group

OVERVIEW

This is a strategy for obtaining ongoing feedback during any multisession class. All too often, teachers solicit student feedback after the course is over—too late to make any adjustments.

PROCEDURE

1. Establish after-class times when you would like to obtain feedback from students.
2. Ask for a small group of volunteers to meet with you. Tell them their job is to solicit the reactions of other students before the meeting time.
3. Use questions such as these:

   - What has been helpful? Unhelpful?
   - Which have been unclear?
   - What would help you to learn better?
   - Are you ready to move on to new material?
   - Am I relating the material enough to your life?
   - What would you like more of at our next class?
   - What would you like less of?
   - What would you like to continue?

VARIATIONS

1. Try out a teaching strategy with the "advisory group" that you are planning to use for the entire class. Obtain reactions.
2. Use other alternatives for obtaining ongoing feedback, such as postmeeting reaction surveys or an oral survey of student reactions.

4

How to Make Learning Unforgettable

Some teachers teach until the final moments of a school term, semester, or course of study. They think that, at the last minute, they can cram in more information and cover topics and material that are still on their agenda.

The value of "covering" any subject is suspect. To *cover* means to hide, to disguise—and in some cases, to scatter about. The urge to teach until the end often leads to hiding, disguising, and scattering about. When learning is active, by contrast, there is an opportunity for *understanding*. When time is taken to consolidate what has been learned, there is an opportunity for *retention*.

Think about what happens when you work hard at a computer, retrieving information, solving problems, and composing thoughts—but, you fail to save the work you've done. Yep—it's all gone. Learning, too, can vanish if students are not given the chance to save what they have learned.

Besides *saving* what has been learned, it's also important to *savor* it. Like any experience, learning is savored when there is a chance to reflect on it and give it emotional closure. Just as we have spoken of the "appetizer" and the "entrée" portion of active learning, we now can consider the "dessert."

There are many positive actions you can take to bring your class to a meaningful and, perhaps, even unforgettable close. In this section, we will consider them in four categories.

1. **Reviewing Strategies:** This part deals with ways to help students recall what they have learned and test their current knowledge and ability. You will find reviewing strategies that engage students and help them "save" the learning they have acquired.

2. **Self-Assessment:** This part deals with ways to help students assess what they now know, what they now can do, and what attitudes they now hold. You will find assessment strategies that help students evaluate their progress.

3. **Future Planning:** This part deals with ways to help students consider what they will do to use what they have learned. You will find

future planning strategies that confront students with the fact that their learning does not stop in the classroom.

4. **Final Sentiments:** This part deals with ways to help students reminisce about their experiences together and express appreciations. You will find strategies that help to bring closure to the class and enable students to say goodbye.

Reviewing Strategies

One of the surest ways to make learning stick is to include time for reviewing what has been learned. Material that has been reviewed **by students** is likely to be retained five times as much as material that has not. That's because reviewing allows students to reconsider the information and find ways to store it in their brains.

What follows is an array of strategies to promote review. In addition to being active, they all make reviewing fun.

79

Index Card Match

OVERVIEW

This is an active, fun way to review class material. It allows students to pair up and quiz their classmates.

PROCEDURE

1. On separate index cards, write down questions about anything taught in the class. Create enough question cards to equal one-half the number of students.
2. On separate cards, write answers to each of these questions.
3. Mix the two sets of cards and shuffle them several times so that they are well mixed.
4. Give out one card to each student. Explain that this is a matching exercise. Some students have review questions and others have the answers.
5. Have students find their matching cards. When a match is formed, ask the matching students to find seats together. (Tell them not to reveal to other students what is contained on their cards.)
6. When all the matching pairs have seated, have each pair quiz the rest of the class by reading aloud their question and challenging classmates to tell them the answer.

VARIATIONS

1. Develop cards containing a sentence with a missing word to be matched to cards containing the missing word—for example, "The president is the _____ of the armed forces. *(commander-in-chief)*."
2. Develop cards containing questions with several possible answers—for example, "What are ways to defuse a conflict?" Match them with cards that contain a corresponding assortment of answers. When each pair quizzes the group, have them obtain several answers from other students.

80

Topical Review

OVERVIEW

This strategy gently challenges students to recall what was learned in each of the topics or units of the class. It is an excellent way to help students revisit the content you have covered.

PROCEDURE

1. At the end of a class, present students with a list of the topics you have covered. Explain that you want to find out what they remember about them and what they have forgotten. Keep the atmosphere informal so that they will not feel threatened by the activity.

2. Ask students to recall what each topic was about and as many things as they can remember about it. Ask questions such as these:

   - What does this topic refer to?
   - Why is it important?
   - Who can give me an example of what we learned in this topic?
   - What value does this topic have for you?
   - What were some of the learning activities we experienced with each topic?

   If little is recalled, handle their forgetting humorously, or blame yourself for not making the topic "unforgettable."

3. Continue in chronological order until you have touched on all the course material (or as much of it as you have time and student interest).

4. As you proceed through the content, make any final remarks you wish.

VARIATIONS

1. Have partners or subgroups discuss each topic with one another instead of using a full-class process.

2. If there are ten or fewer students, invite them to gather around a list of the course topics on a chalkboard or flip chart and conduct their own review of the material. To give them the sense that the review is not a test, consider leaving the room while the process is going on. This will empower them to use the time as they see fit.

81
Giving Questions and Getting Answers

OVERVIEW

This is a team-building strategy to involve students in the review of learning material from a previous class or at the end of a course.

PROCEDURE

1. Hand out two index cards to each student.
2. Ask each student to complete the following sentences:

   Card 1: I still have a question about _____ .

   Card 2: I can answer a question about _____ .

3. Create subgroups and have each subgroup select the most pertinent "question to ask" and the most interesting "question to answer" from the cards of their group members.
4. Ask each subgroup to report the "question to ask" it has selected. Determine if anyone in the full class can answer the question. If not, the teacher should respond.
5. Ask each subgroup to report the "question to answer" it has selected. Have subgroup members share the answer with the rest of the class.

VARIATIONS

1. Prepare, in advance, several question cards, and distribute them to subgroups. Ask subgroups to choose one or more questions that they are capable of answering.
2. Prepare, in advance, several answer cards and distribute them to subgroups. Ask subgroups to choose one or more answers that they find helpful in reviewing what they have learned.

82
Crossword Puzzle

OVERVIEW

Designing a review test as a crossword puzzle invites immediate engagement and participation. A crossword puzzle can be completed individually or in teams.

PROCEDURE

1. The first step is to brainstorm several key terms or names related to the course of study you have completed.
2. Construct a simple crossword puzzle, including as many of these items as you can. Darken spaces you do not need. (*Note:* If it is too difficult to create a crossword puzzle with these items, include fun items, not related to the class, as fillers.)
3. Create clues for your crossword items. Use any of the following kinds:

   - A short definition ("a test used to establish reliability")
   - A category in which the item fits ("a kind of gas")
   - An example ("the phrase *a pleasant peace* is an example of this")
   - An opposite ("the opposite of democracy")

4. Distribute the puzzle to students, either individually or in teams.
5. Set a time limit. Award a prize to the individual or team with the most correct items.

VARIATIONS

1. Have the entire group work cooperatively to complete the crossword puzzle.
2. Simplify the puzzle by deciding on one word that has been key to the entire course. Write it in horizontal crossword squares. Use words that summarize other points in the training session and fit them vertically into the key word.

83
Jeopardy Review

OVERVIEW

This strategy is designed like the popular TV game show—answers are given, and the challenge is to come up with the correct question. The format can easily be used as a review of course material.

PROCEDURE

1. Create three to six categories of review questions. Use any of the following generic categories:

   - Concepts or Ideas
   - Facts
   - Skills
   - Names

   Or create categories by topic. For example, a course on French might involve topics such as *months, numbers,* and *colors.*

2. Develop at least three answers (and their corresponding questions) per category. For example, the answer "This color wine is usually served at room temperature" can be matched to the question "What is **rouge?**" You don't need to have the same number of questions and answers in each category, but you should develop questions and answers of increasing difficulty.

3. Show a Jeopardy game board on a piece of large paper. Announce the categories and the point values for each category. Following is a sample game board:

Months	*Colors*	*Numbers*
10 points	10 points	10 points
20 points	20 points	20 points
30 points	30 points	30 points

4. Form teams of three to six students and provide a responder card for each team. If possible, create groups with a range of skill or knowledge levels.

5. Ask teams to choose a team captain and team scorekeeper.

   - **Team captains** represent the team. They are the only ones who can hold up the responder card and give an answer. **Team captains must confer with the team before giving an answer.**
   - **Scorekeepers** are responsible for adding and subtracting points for their team.

Note: As the game moderator, you are responsible for keeping track of which questions have been asked. As each question is used, cross it off the game board. Put a check mark next to any questions students had difficulty answering. You can come back to these questions when the game is over.

6. Review the following rules of the game:

    - The team captain who holds up the responder card first gets the opportunity to answer.
    - All answers must be given in the form of a question.
    - If the correct response is given, the point value for that category is awarded. If the response is incorrect, the point value is deducted from the team's score, and the other teams have an opportunity to answer.
    - The team that gives the last correct response controls the board.

VARIATIONS

1. Instead of using team captains, have each member of the team take a turn playing Jeopardy. He or she cannot consult with team members before answering.
2. Have students create Jeopardy questions.

84
College Bowl

OVERVIEW

This strategy is a twist on the standard review of material. It allows the teacher to evaluate the extent to which students have mastered the material, and serves to reinforce, clarify, and summarize key points.

PROCEDURE

1. Divide the students into teams of three or four members. Have each team select a name of a college (or sports team, company, car, etc.) they represent.
2. Give each student an index card. Students will hold up their cards to indicate they want a chance to answer a question. The format of the game is a toss-up: Every time you ask a question, any member of any team can indicate his or her desire to answer.
3. Explain the following rules:

   - To answer a question, raise your card.
   - You can raise your card before a question has been fully stated if you think you know the answer. As soon as you interrupt, the statement of the question is stopped.
   - Teams score one point for each member's correct response.
   - When someone answers incorrectly, another team gets to answer. (They can hear the entire question if the other team has interrupted the reading.)

4. After all of the questions have been asked, tally the scores and announce a winner.
5. Based on the responses from the game, review any material that is unclear or that needs reinforcement.

VARIATIONS

1. Alternate questions to each team instead of using a toss-up format.
2. Use the game to test whether students can perform a skill correctly rather than answer a knowledge question.

85

Student Recap

OVERVIEW

This strategy gives students the opportunity to summarize what they have learned and to present their summary to others. It is a good way to get students to recap what they have learned on their own.

PROCEDURE

1. Explain to students that for you to provide a summary of the class would be contrary to the principle of active learning.
2. Divide students into groups of two to four members.
3. Ask each group to create their own summary of the class session. Encourage them to create an outline, a mind map, or any other device that will enable them to communicate the summary to others.
4. Use any of the following questions to guide their work:

   - What were the major topics we have examined?
   - What were some of the key points raised in today's class?
   - What experiences have you had today? What did you get out of them?
   - What ideas or suggestions are you taking away from this class?

5. Invite groups to share their summaries. Applaud their efforts.

VARIATIONS

1. Provide a topical outline of the day and ask students to fill in the details of what was covered.
2. Ask students to set the recap to music. Have them use the melody of a well-known song or let them create a musical rap.

86

Bingo Review

OVERVIEW

This strategy helps to reinforce terms that students have learned in a course of study. It uses the format of a Bingo game.

PROCEDURE

1. Develop a set of 24 or 25 questions about your subject matter that can be answered by a standard term used in your course of study. Here are some example terms:

   - least common denominator
   - hieroglyphics
   - inflation
   - autocracy
   - database
   - Hammurabi code
   - byte

   - latitude
   - impressionism
   - allegory
   - photosynthesis
   - ordinal number
   - schizophrenia
   - subjunctive clause

   You can also use names instead of terms. Here are some examples:

   - Freud
   - Caesar
   - Blake
   - Roosevelt
   - Marco Polo
   - Joan of Arc
   - Dewey

   - Copernicus
   - Pasteur
   - Van Gogh
   - Curie
   - Chaucer
   - Russell
   - Ailey

2. Sort the questions into five piles. Label each pile with the letters B-I-N-G-O. Create Bingo cards for each student. These should be exactly like traditional Bingo cards, with numbers in each of the 24 cells in the 5 × 5 matrix (the middle cell is "Free.")

3. Read a question with an associated number. If a student has the number and can correctly write in the answer, he or she can fill in the cell.

4. Whenever a student achieves five correct answers in a row (either vertically, horizontally, or diagonally), the student may call out "Bingo." Play may continue until all 25 cells are filled.

VARIATIONS

1. Provide an inexpensive prize, such as a piece of candy, whenever students obtain Bingo.
2. Create cards that have the cells previously filled in with 24 of the key terms (plus a "free" cell in the middle). Whenever a question is read, if the student believes that one of the answers on the card fits the question, he or she can simply write in the question number next to it.

87
Hollywood Squares Review

OVERVIEW

This reviewing strategy is based on the once popular TV quiz show **Hollywood Squares.**

PROCEDURE

1. Ask each student to write two or three questions pertaining to the class subject matter. Questions can be in multiple-choice, true/false, or fill-in-the-blanks formats.
2. Collect the questions. If you wish, add a few of your own.
3. Simulate the tic-tac-toe game show format used on *Hollywood Squares.* Set three chairs at the front of the class. Ask three volunteers to sit on the floor in front of the chairs, three to sit in the chairs, and three to stand behind them.
4. Give each of the nine "celebrities" a card with an X printed on one side and an O on the other to tape to their bodies as questions are answered successfully.
5. Ask for two volunteers to serve as contestants. The contestants pick members of the "celebrity" squares to answer the game's questions.
6. Ask the contestants questions in turns. The contestants respond with "agree" or "disagree" to the panel's response as they try to form a tic-tac-toe.
7. Remaining students not involved in the game are given cards that say "agree" on one side and "disagree" on the other to flash to contestants to aid in their decision making.

VARIATIONS

1. Rotate the "celebrities."
2. Pair up students. Have them play tic-tac-toe against each other, based on their ability to answer your review questions.

Self-Assessment

The end of a term, semester, or course of study is a time for reflection. What have I learned? What do I now believe? What are my skills? What do I need to improve? Allowing time for self-assessment gives students the opportunity to examine what the class has meant or done to them. The strategies that follow are structured ways to promote this kind of self-assessment. They also provide a meaningful closure to the class experience.

88
Reconsidering

OVERVIEW

One of the most effective ways to design a unit or course of study is to ask students to state their views about the class topic right at the beginning and then to reassess these views at the end. There are several ways to accomplish this form of reconsideration.

PROCEDURE

1. At the beginning of a unit or course of study, ask students to express their views about the topic. For example, ask about:

   - What makes a _____ effective (e.g., term paper)
   - What is the value of a _____ (e.g., constitution)
   - What advice they would give themselves to be _____ (e.g., better actors)
   - What solutions they could devise in dealing with a problem you pose (e.g., how to keep economic growth in check)

   Use any one of the following formats:

   - Group discussion
   - A questionnaire
   - An opening debate
   - A written statement

2. At the end of a unit or course of study, ask students to express their views again.
3. Ask students whether their views have remained the same or have shifted.

VARIATIONS

1. Discuss the factors that created shifts in viewpoints.
2. Begin the course with an exercise in which students write down recent situations in which they were not as skillful or knowledgeable as they would have liked to be. End the course with an exercise in which students ask themselves how they would handle these situations more effectively in the future.

89

Return on Your Investment

OVERVIEW

This approach asks students to assess whether they have profited from the class. It places them in the position of "owning" their own learning expectations rather than merely going along for the ride.

PROCEDURE

1. At the beginning of a class, ask students to write down what they hope to get out of the class. Here are some ways to structure this exercise:

   • Ask students to list their own learning goals for the class.
   • Ask students to list what they have found difficult or uninteresting about the subject matter.
   • Ask students to list ways in which they might be able to use what they learn.

2. Periodically, set aside some time to allow students to read their initial statement and consider what value the class has had for them thus far.
3. At the end of the term, semester, or course of study, ask students to assess whether their investment of time and effort in the class has been worthwhile in light of their initial hopes.
4. Obtain feedback from students.

VARIATIONS

1. Create a visual display of students' goals so that they can refer to them easily throughout the session.
2. Ask students to assign a percentage that describes their return on investment in the class (ROI). For example, a student who felt the class was worthwhile might indicate that he or she had received a 75 percent return on investment. (Sounds pretty good!)

90
Gallery of Learning

OVERVIEW

This activity is a way to assess and celebrate what students have learned over a course of study.

PROCEDURE

1. Divide students into groups of two to four members.
2. Ask each subgroup to discuss what its members are taking away from the class. These may include any of the following:

   - New knowledge
   - New skills
   - Improvement in _____ (e.g. , programming skills)
   - New or renewed interest in _____ (e.g., poetry)
   - Confidence in _____ (e.g., speaking German)

   Then ask them to list on large paper these "learnings." Ask them to title the list "What We Are Taking Away."
3. Paper the walls with these lists.
4. Ask students to walk by each list. Ask that each person place a check mark next to learnings on lists other than his or her own that he or she is taking away as well.
5. Survey the results, noting the most popular learnings. Also mention some that are unusual and unexpected.

VARIATIONS

1. If the size of the class warrants, ask each student to make his or her own list.
2. Instead of listing "learnings," ask students to list "keepers"—ideas or suggestions given in the class that students think are worth keeping or retaining for future application.

91
Physical Self-Assessment

OVERVIEW

This activity is similar to Activity 66, "Active Self-Assessment." Using it at the end of a class allows students to assess how much they have learned or to modify previously held beliefs.

PROCEDURE

1. Create one or more statements that assess student change. Examples might include:

   - I have changed my views about _____ due to this class.
   - I have improved my skill(s) in _____ .
   - I have learned new information and concepts.

2. Clear away the chairs or desks to one side and ask the students to stand in the back of the room.

3. Create a rating scale of numbers from 1 through 5 in the front of the room by using the blackboard or posting numbers on the wall.

4. Explain that a statement will be read to the class. After hearing each one, the student should stand in front of the rating number that best matches his or her self-assessment. Use the following scale:
   1 = strongly disagree
   2 = disagree
   3 = not sure
   4 = agree
   5 = strongly agree

5. As each statement is read, students should move to the place in the room that best matches their self-assessment. **Encourage students to assess themselves realistically.** Point out that several factors might create little or no change. They include previous knowledge or skill level, the need for more practice or time, and so forth.

6. After lines form in front of the various positions, invite some students to share why they have chosen that rating. Underscore their honesty.

7. After hearing others' opinions, invite anyone who wishes to alter their position on the scale to do so.

VARIATIONS

1. Utilize a private paper-and-pencil self-assessment instead of creating a public exercise.
2. Ask students to line up in order of how much they agree with each statement. This technique, called a "physical continuum," forces students to discuss with each other what they have learned or how they have changed as they jockey for their preferred position on the continuum.

92

Assessment Collage

OVERVIEW

This exercise uses the activity of making a picture collage to enable students to assess themselves in a creative way.

PROCEDURE

1. Gather several magazines. Have scissors, marking pens, and glue (or cellophane tape) available for students.
2. Ask students to create a collage that represents what they have learned and/or how they have changed in the class.
3. Make the following suggestions:

    -   Cut out words from magazine advertisements that describe your current views, skills, or knowledge.
    -   Paste visual images that graphically describe your accomplishments.
    -   Use marking pens to title the collage and to add your own words or images.

4. Create a gallery of the assessment collages. Invite students to tour the results and comment on the collages displayed.

VARIATIONS

1. Create team collages instead of individual ones.
2. Instead of a collage, have students create a "shield" or "coat of arms" that displays their accomplishments.

Future Planning

At the conclusion of any class that has featured active learning, students will naturally ask, "Now what?" The success of active learning is really measured by how that question is answered—that is, how what has been learned in the class affects what students will do in the future. The strategies that follow are designed to promote future planning. Some are fairly quick techniques you can use when time is limited. Others require more time and commitment but lead to even better results.

93

Keep On Learning

OVERVIEW

This strategy enables students to brainstorm ways to continue learning on their own the subject you have taught them.

PROCEDURE

1. Point out your hope that your students' learning won't stop simply because the class is over.
2. Suggest to students that there are many ways for them to continue learning on their own.
3. Indicate that one way to do this is to brainstorm their own list of ideas to "keep on learning."
4. Create subgroups. Have each subgroup brainstorm ideas. Here are some all-purpose suggestions:

   - Look for subject-related articles in newspapers, magazines, and so forth.
   - Take another course in the same subject area.
   - Create a future reading list.
   - Reread books and review notes taken in class.
   - Teach something you've learned to someone else.
   - Get a job or take an assignment that uses the skills you have learned.

5. Reconvene the class and ask each subgroup to share its best ideas.

VARIATIONS

1. Prepare in advance, a list of suggestions for the students. Ask them to check those they feel would be suitable for them.
2. Send students ideas to extend their learning a few weeks after the class is over.

94
Bumper Stickers

OVERVIEW

This enjoyable strategy enables students to create reminders to use what they have learned. They place these reminders on signs that they can attach to any surface (refrigerator, door, desk, etc.).

PROCEDURE

1. Invite students to create imaginary bumper stickers they might place on the car that advertise:

    - One thing they have learned in the class ("Observation is the basis for all science")
    - A key thought or piece of advice they will keep in mind to guide them in the future ("Use topic sentences")
    - An action step they will take in the future ("Preview what you read before you read it")
    - A question to ponder ("What is my goal?")

2. Urge students to express themselves as concisely as possible. Have them brainstorm possibilities before making their selections. Encourage them to obtain reactions to their ideas from others. They might want to base their signs on well-known bumper stickers, such as "Honk if you _____," or advertising slogans, such as "_____ . No book can match it."

3. Provide materials and supplies to make the bumper stickers as attractive as possible.

4. Make a gallery display of the stickers. Make sure students take home their own stickers to display as they see fit.

VARIATIONS

1. Provide students with stickers made by you to take with them.

2. Have students come up with bumper sticker ideas on index cards. Gather the cards and pass them around the group. Have each student select three ideas from other members of the class that will serve them well.

95
I Hereby Resolve

OVERVIEW

This is a widely practiced strategy for gaining commitment to applying what has been learned in a class. It also is an excellent way to help students remember the class long after it is over.

PROCEDURE

1. Ask students to tell you what they are taking away from the class. Record their thoughts and display them as a composite list.
2. Give students a blank sheet of paper and an envelope.
3. Invite them to write themselves a letter indicating what they (personally) are taking away from the class and what steps they intend to take to use what they have learned or continue to learn more about the subject on their own. Suggest that they could begin the letter with the words "I hereby resolve."
4. Inform them that the letter is confidential. Ask them to place it in the envelope, address it to themselves, and seal the envelope.
5. Ask the students to place a Post-it™ note on the envelope with the date on which they want you to mail it to them. Promise to send the letters to the students when they have requested.

VARIATIONS

1. Instead of having the students write to themselves, suggest that they write to someone else, indicating their resolve and asking for support.
2. After one month, send a letter to students with a summary of the main points of the class. Encourage them to apply what they have learned. Suggest ways to continue learning about the subject matter.

96
Follow-Up Questionnaire

OVERVIEW

This is a clever strategy for raising students' consciousness about the class long after it is over. It also serves as a way to stay in touch with students.

PROCEDURE

1. Explain to students that you would like to send them a follow-up questionnaire one month from now. The questionnaire is intended (1) to help them assess what they have learned and how well they are doing in using it and (2) to give you feedback.
2. Urge them to fill out the questionnaire for their own benefit. Ask them to return the questionnaire if they so desire.
3. When you develop the questionnaire, consider the following suggestions:

   - Keep the tone informal and friendly.
   - Mix the questions so that the easiest to fill out come first. Use formats such as checklists, rating scales, incomplete sentences, and a short essay.
   - Ask about what they remember the most, what skills they are currently using, and what success they have had.
   - Offer students the opportunity to call you with questions and application problems.

   Here is an example:

   After participating in a class on "Assertive Communication," students are sent this follow-up questionnaire:

   Hello! How are things going? I hope you have had the opportunity to work on your assertive communication skills. As I promised, I'm sending you this questionnaire to help you review and assess your ability to assert yourself to obtain the goals you are seeking. By sending this questionnaire back to me, you will also help me to evaluate the impact of the class.
   Thanks!

   1. Please rank the following situations in order of difficulty to you on a scale from 1 (least difficult) to 5 (most important).

      _____ Saying "No" without apologizing

      _____ Initiating a conversation

_____ Stating my feelings honestly

_____ Being persuasive

_____ Handling very difficult people

2. Indicate the degree of difficulty you have in the following situations:

	Easy	Somewhat Difficult	Very Difficult
Talking with the opposite sex	_____	_____	_____
Disciplining children	_____	_____	_____
Talking on the telephone	_____	_____	_____
Asking for a raise	_____	_____	_____
Talking in a group	_____	_____	_____
Resisting salespeople	_____	_____	_____
Returning food in a restaurant	_____	_____	_____

3. Briefly describe a recent situation in which you acted assertively:

_____

_____

4. Describe a recent situation in which you did not act assertively and regretted it:

_____

_____

5. Check one of these statements:

_____ Please call me. I'm having difficulty with _____ .

_____ Everything's going well. There's no need to contact me.

VARIATIONS

1. Send follow-up handouts that might be of interest to students.
2. Instead of sending a questionnaire, interview students by phone or in person. Use a small sample if the class was large.

97
Sticking to It

OVERVIEW

This is a procedure in which students make a serious commitment to apply what they have learned.

PROCEDURE

1. Ask students to fill out a follow-up form at the end of the class containing statements as to how they plan to apply what they have learned or to continue learning more about the subject. Here is a sample form.

Future Planning Form

Describe how you plan to apply this course and tell when and how you plan to apply it. Be specific.

A. Situation: _____

_____

My plan to apply: _____

_____

_____

B. Situation: _____

_____

My plan to apply: _____

_____

_____

Describe what you want to do to continue learning about (insert subject):

_____

_____

_____

_____

_____

_____

_____

2. When the form is completed, inform the students that their future planning sheet will be sent to them in three to four weeks. At that time, they are sent these follow-up instructions.

   Please review your future planning sheet. Place the letter A next to those plans you have been able to apply successfully. Place the letter B next to those plans you are still working on applying. Place the letter C next to those plans you have not been able to do anything about. Explain what obstacles stopped your application.

VARIATIONS

1. Have students share their future plans immediately with an advisor. Suggest that they work together on a plan to help the student "stick to it."
2. Enlist the advisors' support of this plan **before** the class even begins.

Final Sentiments

In many classes, students develop feelings of closeness toward other classmates. This is especially true if the students have taken part in active learning activities. They need to say "goodbye" to each other and express their appreciation for the support and encouragement given each other during the class. There are many ways to help facilitate these final sentiments. The strategies that follow are some good ones.

98
Goodbye Scrabble

OVERVIEW

This is a technique that enables students to join together at the end of a class and celebrate what they have experienced together. This is achieved by creating a giant Scrabble board.

PROCEDURE

1. Create a large display of the title of the course or subject matter. Merge the words in the title if there are more than one. For example, "ancient history" becomes *ancienthistory.*
2. Give students marking pens. Explain, if necessary, how words can be created in Scrabble fashion, using the displayed title as a base. Review the ways that words can be created:

    - Horizontally or vertically
    - Beginning with, ending with, and incorporating any available letters

    Remind students, however, that two words cannot merge with each other—there must be a space between them. Permit proper names as words.
3. Set a time limit and invite students to create as many key words as they can **that are associated with the subject matter or the learning experiences that have taken place.**
4. Suggest that they divide up the labor so that some students are recording while others are searching for new words.
5. Call "time" and have the students count up the words and applaud the stunning visual record of their experience with one another!

VARIATIONS

1. If the group size is unwieldy for this activity, divide the class into subgroups that each create a Scrabble board. Display the results together and tally the **total** number of words produced by the entire class.
2. Simplify the activity by writing the course title or subject matter vertically and asking students to write (horizontally) a verb, adjective, or noun that they associate with the title and that begins with each letter.

99

Connections

OVERVIEW

This is an activity that symbolically draws a class to a close. It is especially appropriate when students have formed close connections with each other.

PROCEDURE

1. Use a skein of yarn to connect students, literally and symbolically.
2. Ask everyone to stand and form a circle. Start the process by stating briefly what you have experienced as a result of facilitating the class.
3. Holding onto the end of the yarn, toss the skein to a student on the other side of the circle. Ask that person to state briefly what he or she has experienced as a result of participating in the class. Than ask that person to hold onto the yarn and toss the skein to another student.
4. Have each student take a turn at receiving the skein, sharing reflections, and tossing the yarn on, continuing to hold on his or her piece. The resulting visual is a web of yarn connecting every member of the group.

    Some of the comments that might be expressed include:

    - *I'm glad I got to know people on a personal level.*
    - *I feel that I can be open and honest with everyone here.*
    - *I had fun in this class.*
    - *I'm going to think of ways to practice what I learned here.*
    - *You all have been a great group!*

5. Complete the activity by stating that the program began as a collection of individuals willing to connect and learn from each other.
6. Cut the yarn with scissors so that each person, though departing as an individual, takes a piece of the other students with him or her. Thank students for their interest, ideas, time, and effort.

VARIATIONS

1. Ask each student to express appreciation to the person who tossed him or her the yarn.
2. Instead of using yarn, toss a ball or another similar object. As each person receives the ball, he or she can express final sentiments.

100

Class Photo

OVERVIEW

This is an activity that acknowledges the contributions of every student while at the same time celebrating the total class.

PROCEDURE

1. Assemble students for a class photograph. It's best to create at least three rows—one row sitting on the floor, one row sitting in chairs, and one row standing behind the chairs. As you are about to take their picture, express your own final sentiments. Stress how much active learning depends on the support and involvement of students. Thank students for playing such a large part in the success of the class.
2. Then, invite one student at a time to leave the group and become the "photographer." (*Optional:* Have each participant merely come up and view what a final picture of the class would look like.)
3. If the class is not too large, ask each student to share his or her final thoughts with the group. Ask the group to applaud the student for his or her contributions to the group.
4. When the film is developed, give each member his or her own photograph of the class.

VARIATIONS

1. Use the photography session as an opportunity to review some of the highlights of the program.
2. Instead of a public disclosure of sentiments, ask students to write final thoughts on sheets of paper taped to the walls.

101

The Final Exam

OVERVIEW

This is a fun way to reminisce about the activities that took place in the class.

PROCEDURE

1. Give students a blank sheet of paper and tell them it is time for their "final exam." Keep them in suspense about the exam.
2. Tell them that their task is to write down, in order, the many active learning activities they have experienced in the class. (At this point, reveal that this is a fun challenge that will not be graded.)
3. After each student has finished (or given up!), generate a classwide list. Make adjustments until the correct list is obtained.
4. With the list in view, ask students to reminisce about these experiences, recalling moments of fun, cooperation, and insight.
5. Facilitate the discussion so that the exchange of memories brings a strong emotional closure to the class.

VARIATIONS

1. Provide a list of the activities from the beginning. Start the reminiscing discussion immediately.
2. Rather than focusing on activities, focus the exercise on "moments to remember." Leave this phrase open to interpretation. This may create a laughter-filled and perhaps nostalgic review of the class.